THE COMPLETE

BODYBUILDING COOKBOOK

300 | DELICIOUS RECIPES TO BUILD MUSCLE, BURN FAT AND SAVE TIME

JASON FARLEY / RYAN POWELL

Carrillo Press

ISBN-13: 978-1911364139
ISBN-10: 1911364138

CONTENTS

1) DIET AND NUTRITION

When we start on our bodybuilding journey, we must remember that it doesn't matter how strict you are with your training regime, how many reps you can do, or how heavy you can lift - if you are not eating a healthy, balanced diet with the right amount of protein, fats and carbohydrates, then all of your hard work at the gym will be in vain.

Unfortunately, most people sign up for a gym membership and go ahead and pump away, without understanding the need for proper nutrition. More often than not, they spend a lot of time, energy, and money before winding up with zero results and blaming it on external factors such as genetics, poor equipment, and even poor personal trainers!

A common misconception about bodybuilding is that all fuel is good fuel. People may think that it's all about the calorie intake - they've got to eat as much as possible to bulk up and turn it into muscle -but it isn't quite as easy as that.

Energy is used for everything we do in life – walking, working, running, talking, and yes, bodybuilding. But you also need energy for things that we sometimes take for granted. When you sleep, you still breath, your blood still pumps as your heart works, and you still expend energy. To expend energy, human beings need fuel. Think of an automobile needing gasoline to run. Without gasoline, it won't start, much less drive anywhere. Your body works in the same way, but unlike cars that don't use up energy when they're in the garage overnight, your body uses up tons of energy while you're sleeping!

If you want to get the ultimate body, the fuel that you put into it needs to be just right. This is why nutrition is so important. As previously mentioned, sometimes people can actually wind up sabotaging their own training plans exactly because they don't know what to eat. Moreover, the things they do eat, instead of helping them build muscle mass, cause them to lose muscle, weight and energy. There goes the bodybuilding goals! Keep reading to learn more about the diet and what is important to consider.

CALORIES

Each calorie is a unit of energy. If you don't consume enough calories, the activity in your brain actually slows down and you lose energy. If you consume too many calories, this will lead to weight gain and the many health problems related to that condition.

It is important therefore to know how many calories you should be eating, taking into consideration your gender, exercise regime and body building goals. Frayn's text on metabolic regulation lists the following formula:

Energy intake (food) = Energy expended (heat + work) + Energy stored

Look at it this way: it's the beginning of your training day, and you eat a balanced breakfast, which means that you'll be eating a specific number of calories. When these calories enter your body, the following things can happen to them:

- Some will be stored as fat (meaning energy you can use in the future),
- Some will be transferred into your body's cells to be converted into the energy that you need to get through your exercises,
- Some will be immediately converted into heat.

The challenge is to make sure that you know how many calories you'll need to eat, and where you'll be getting those calories from: some must be used immediately so you can jump right into your workout; some must be stored for use over the rest of the day; and some must be used so that your body itself can keep going.

The level of your energy balance is the balance between the calories you consume and those that you burn through physical activity. What you eat is INCOMING ENERGY, and what you burn up through physical activity is OUTGOING

ENERGY.

Energy Balance = Energy Intake - Energy Expenditure

So -

If ENERGY IN (calories eaten) and ENERGY OUT (calories burned) are the same over time = your weight stays the same.

If ENERGY IN (calories eaten) are less than ENERGY OUT (calories burned) over time = you will lose weight. This is also called NEGATIVE ENERGY BALANCE.

If ENERGY IN (calories eaten) are more than ENERGY OUT (calories burned) over time = your weight will increase. This is also called POSITIVE ENERGY BALANCE.

To further help you understand what your food is made up of and what you need to be consuming you need to know about macronutrients (the nutrients we need for cell growth, cell repair, energy usage and to maintain bodily functions). There are three basic sources of fuel that provide energy:

PROTEIN

Protein molecules are the building blocks for muscle; the object of our bodybuilding efforts. All of the cells in your body contain protein. Protein is made up of amino acids and is used to resupply, rebuild, and repair muscle cells and also perform a wide range of other functions in your body, including the replication of DNA, transporting molecules, responding to stimuli, and catalyzing metabolic reactions. Over 2/3 of protein in your body resides in your muscles.

Proteins come in a variety of forms including animal sources (meats, dairy products, fish, and eggs) as well as plant sources including nuts (almonds, cashew nuts, walnuts), legumes (peas, beans, lentils) and grains (corn, wheat, oats). Most people will consume the recommended amount of protein by eating a balanced diet. Depending on your goals though, it might be necessary to increase your intake of protein using supplements such as protein powders.

CARBOHYDRATES

Carbohydrates are used by the body as the first and most accessible source of energy. Again, they come in many forms (some better for us than others) and include the following amongst others:

- Grains (rice and wheat)
- Fruits (most contain fructose)
- Milk
- Vegetables
- Table sugar, and Splenda (sucrose)
- Candy and syrup
- Beans and legumes

When carbohydrates are ingested, they are converted into blood glucose through the process of glycolysis, before being absorbed through the small intestines and then entering the bloodstream; this causes blood glucose levels to rise. This process of making and transporting glucose triggers a very important hormonal action - the pancreas makes insulin, a peptide that helps take the sugar to the cells so that they can use it as energy. This metabolic process is essential but can go wrong when we eat too many carbohydrates or sugars.

When there is too much glucose in the bloodstream, the pancreas secretes more insulin. This moves excess glucose in the blood to other tissues, for instance the muscles, to be stored in the form of glycogen. Excess glycogen is then pushed into fat cells for storage. If there's enough glucose in the body, it is the preferred fuel for most tissues, but any excess amount is embedded into muscle tissue, leading to excess fat stores. Carbohydrate fuel needs constant re-supply to give the human body a feeling of being satiated or "full."

Carbohydrates are the human body's key source of energy. Without glucose, both the body and the brain itself would slow down and become impaired. However, it is the processed carbohydrates that we need to watch out for as these have led to a variety of illnesses prevalent today.

THE GLYCEMIC INDEX

GI measures the extent to which a food carbohydrate can be classified as simple or complex. This classification is based on the food's chemical composition as well as how quickly the sugars in the food are synthesized and absorbed in your body. The GI measures how a given food product affects the blood sugar levels; it measures the relative rise in the raise of blood sugar levels following the consumption of that food product. Simple carbohydrates break down more easily during the process of digestion, which means that high levels of glucose enter the body in a short period of time. These products e.g. white bread, white rice, cornflakes, certain processed breakfast cereals and peeled white potatoes, tend to have high glycemic indexes.

The opposite is true for food products made with complex carbohydrates: it takes a longer time for these to be broken down by the body, resulting in a gradual and more controlled release of glucose into the blood. These products tend to have low glycemic indexes: beans, fruits and vegetables, and mushrooms fall into this category.

In the long term, and in the context of your bodybuilding goals, consuming low-GI foods is more beneficial: what you get is a controlled release of energy over a longer period of time, which means you can do more, lift more, and come out on top in terms of your health.

FATS

Although this sounds like a taboo word in the bodybuilding world, or for anyone looking to get fit for that matter, the human body actually needs certain kinds of fats in order to survive. We store energy in the form of fat so that it can be used as energy.

We do however, need to be aware of the different types of fats: saturated, trans fats and unsaturated. It's been claimed by many health organizations from all over the world that the high intake of saturated fats might be to blame for conditions like cardiovascular disease, diabetes, and certain forms of cancer. Saturated fats are those found in fattier cuts of meat, butter, milk, lard and those in pies, cookies and baked products. You can switch to leaner cuts of meat instead of fatty ones, from full-fat milk to non-fat milk and cut out baked and packaged products as much as possible.

Trans fats are artificial fats, created by a process in the factory. They are found in foods such as packaged foods, margarines, some frying oils and fast foods. Trans fats, increase cholesterol and should be avoided as much as possible.

Unsaturated fats are the fats you should be eating. These are commonly known as 'healthy fats' and are vital to a healthy diet. They include omega-3 and omega-6 fatty acids which are found in fish, shellfish, olive oil, and leafy vegetables.

WATER

Hydration is critical. The human body is composed of at least 60% water and it is contained in literally every cell, every organ, and every system in the human body. It is important to drink lots of water before and during your workouts because water makes it easier for the heart to pump blood and nutrients through the body. Water also helps muscles to move more efficiently.

You might now be wondering about the effectiveness of products like energy drinks and sports drinks, and while they can be useful in providing the electrolytes that you lose during your workouts, these kinds of drinks can be loaded with extra sugars or large amounts of sodium. Use sparingly and not as a replacement for water.

ALCOHOL

Alcohol is a diuretic - it forces your kidneys to do much more work to break it down. This means you will produce more urine and in turn become dehydrated.

Being dehydrated means your muscles grow weaker and you can't tap into your body's energy reserves as efficiently as you normally would. Alcohol has other negative effects on your body: it can actually cause you to lose muscle tissue, because the alcohol disrupts the process of creating and maintaining muscle cells. It's your decision whether you're going to give up alcohol whilst training or not but there is no two ways about it - it will impair the process. I believe moderation is the key.

2) MUSCLE STARTS IN THE KITCHEN

The following are four principles for stocking your kitchen:

PRINCIPLE 1: Whole, fresh foods are better than packaged or processed. Avoid foods with added sugar, salt, fat and preservatives. Switch to cooking methods that don't add salt or fat.

PRINCIPLE 2: Pre-planning is essential. Plan the meals and snacks you will need for the week ahead. Buy as much as you can fresh and freeze what will go off before the end of the week - just remember to take it out 24 hours before cooking to defrost. Fish out or purchase a set of Tupperware boxes that can be used in the microwave. You'll need about 10 containers for meals. Small containers for snacks are a bonus! You'll also benefit from purchasing zip-up sandwich bags, baking paper and/or cooking foil.

PRINCIPLE 3: Buying whole, fresh foods can be more expensive but be savvy and choose markets/grocery stores with better deals and stick to what you need after you've planned to avoid waste.

PRINCIPLE 4: Remove temptations, Look in your kitchen and pantry for processed foods and take them out right now! This includes the following:

- Processed baked goods, including doughnuts,
- Candy,
- Deli meats, such as bacon, pastrami, and ham,
- Potato chips and similar snack food items,
- Fruit juices with added sugar,

- Sugary breakfast cereals.

YOUR GROCERY LIST

Low GI Carbs:

- Whole-wheat bread and pasta,
- Rolled or steel-cut oats -- not the quick-cooking or instant stuff,
- Brown rice,
- Quinoa,
- Sweet potatoes.

Proteins:

- Eggs and egg whites,
- Fatty fish, such as salmon, tuna and sardines,
- Lean fish, such as tilapia, mahi mahi,
- Beef - where possible, choose loin or round cuts,
- Skinless chicken and turkey breasts,
- Lean ground meats (beef, turkey, pork)
- Canned fish - packed in water and not oil,
- Beans -- kidney beans, pinto beans, lima beans etc.,
- Tofu.

Good fats:

- Milk (skimmed),
- Cottage cheese,
- Greek yogurt,
- Olive oil,
- Coconut oil,
- Avocado,
- Whole peanut butter,
- Nuts and seeds.

All fruit and vegetables: Remember to buy your fruits and vegetables when they're in season for maximum taste and optimal nutrition. Alternatively frozen varieties are just as healthy.

Herbs and spices: Choose chili flakes, thyme, oregano, paprika etc. to add flavor to your meals and stop you reaching for the salt.

COOKING AND MEAL PREP ESSENTIALS

1. Baking, boiling, steaming or broiling is better than frying. If frying, use olive oil or coconut oil instead of sunflower or vegetable oils. Olive oil cooking sprays are also great for controlling the amount you use.

2. Set aside one day a week to prepare meals in advance and portion up into containers so that they're ready to go!

3. Cook in bulk and portion up meals. Meat can be kept in the fridge for 2-3 days as well as the carbohydrates and vegetables you prepare. Keep the rest in the freezer and defrost 24 hours in advance of eating. Alternatively prep meals 2 days a week for the following 2-3 days.

4. Know how many meals/snacks you will eat per day in order to prepare.

3) EATING TO BUILD MUSCLE

Let's get this out of the way – going on a diet doesn't mean you are not allowed to eat tasty food. You can, and when you are bulking up, you will be doing a hell of a lot of eating. In lean muscle building, it simply means being mindful of what you eat.

The principle of eating to build muscle is quite similar to eating to lose weight: you need to compute your calorie intake. You need to know how many calories you need to consume in order to successfully build your muscle.

WHY YOU CAN'T GAIN WEIGHT

There is only one major reason behind the lack of weight gain – calorie deficit. Your intake of calories should be greater than the calories you use up.

If you're skinny and you're gunning for gains, it can be frustrating to force yourself to eat, hoping to get bigger. If you're taking in enough calories, then you should gain at least a few pounds, right?

The most obvious factor behind calorie deficit is that you're not eating enough food consistently. You should eat regularly with each meal consisting of quality protein, unsaturated fats, and complex carbs.

HOW MANY CALORIES DO YOU NEED FOR EXTREME MUSCLE GROWTH?

The most important concept in calorie intake is determining what your calorie maintenance level (CML) is. That level is the approximate amount of calorie intake that you need to maintain your weight if you were to eat without exercising. A rough calculation is done by multiplying your current body weight by 15. For example, if you are 200 pounds, your CML will be 3,000 calories per day. Eating 3,000 calories per day will leave you at your current 200-pound level.

If you want to gain muscle, you will need to eat 20% over your CML. This time, you will need to be at a calorie surplus – you need to eat 20% more calories than your CML. In this case, you will need to eat 20% more, or about 600 calories (3,000 times 20%) over your CML. Now you have to make sure that you eat at least 3,600 caloriesper day.

You need to weigh yourself at a selected "starting point" in the week. This should be a morning when you have not yet taken in any food or water. A good starting day would be a Monday morning. You need to monitor what happens to your weight on a weekly basis, and depending on your objectives, you should see the following results if you are counting your calories correctly:

With the objective to gain muscle or increase strength, you should be aiming to gain 2 pounds per month. If you are gaining less than ½ pound a week, or are not gaining any weight at all, you need to increase your calorie intake by another 10%. In the case of the 3,000 calorie per day, 200 pound man, this means increasing calorie intake by another 300 calories per day. On the other hand, if you are gaining more than 2 pounds per month, consider removing 10% (300 calories)

from your daily intake.

HOW MUCH WEIGHT SHOULD YOU BE GAINING EACH WEEK?

Here's an example of how much weight you should gain after training for a year and more. This is from the Lean Muscle Mass Gain Model developed by Lyle McDonald.

Years Training:

1 year	20-25 lbs (2 lbs per month)
2 years	10-12 lbs (1 lbs per month)
3 years	5-6 lbs (0.5 lbs per month)
4 years	2-3 lbs (not worth calculating)

According to this diagram, your weight gain should decrease yearly. Within 4 years of consistent training, you would be able to develop enough muscle that all you need to do then is to maintain your calorie intake and exercise routine.

Lean muscle building macros: How to split calories between protein, carbs and fats:

Protein

As a healthy adult with consistent weight training, you are recommended to follow this daily protein intake:

0.8 to 1.5 grams for every pound of your body weight.

A study recently published in the Journal of Applied Physiology revealed that subjects who ate at least 20 grams of protein spread out over six meals and snacks, lost more body fat, and increased lean mass, more than the average male. And this is without any training at all, accomplished only via diet!

The study showed that protein synthesis was about 25% higher for those subjects who at least 30 grams of protein in each of their three meals, as opposed to those who had most of their protein during dinner.

I recommend that you eat protein six times a day spreading your intake over the day. Six full meals may sound excessive but you need to do this especially in the beginning stages of your program.

(1 gram of protein = 4 calories)

Fat

The recommended fat intake for average adults is about 25% of the total calorie intake.

(1 gram of fat= 9 calories)

So let's say your calorie maintenance level is 2,000 calories per day and 25% of that is 500. That means you should divide 500 by 9 to get the amount of fat that you need per day. According to this example, you will need to consume about 55 grams of fat each day. You can find 'healthy fat' contents in fish, nuts, and seeds.

Carbohydrates

Your ideal carb intake must come from healthy foods like fruits and vegetables, brown or white rice, sweet potatoes, and different types of beans. Unless you have a problem with digesting grains, you may also find the carbs you need in whole grain products.
After you have worked out how many calories you need from your protein and fats, the calories left should come from carbohydrates.

(1g of carbohydrates = 4 calories)

Here, I'm going to show you every step clearly. Let's say I weigh 175 lbs and my calorie maintenance level per day is 2,250 calories. Here's how I would create my diet plan with this number.

1.   Since I want to build muscle, that means I need to add my calorie intake. Since my maintenance level is 2,250 calories, I would need to consume 2,500 calories each day.
2.   Since I weigh 175 lbs, that means I need to consume 175 grams of protein per day. Now, a gram of protein contains 4 calories. So if I multiply 175 by 4, that

means I will already consume 700 calories with 175 grams of protein.

3.   Then, I need to take about 25% of my calorie intake from fat. Since my maintenance calorie level is 2,500 per day, 25% of that is 625. Since I can consume 9 calories in 1 gram of fat, then I would need to consume about 69 grams of fat each day.

4.   By this time, I already have 700 calories from protein and 625 calories from fat, which gives me a total of 1325 calories already. Since I need to take 2,500 calories per day, I still need to consume additional 1117 calories.

5.   Now, my remaining calorie need should come from carbs. Since I can consume 4 calories in 1 gram of carbs, I would need to consume about 294 grams of carbs each day.

So that's it. You have learned the most important parts of the sample diet plan. According to the given example, here's how my diet plan should appear:

1.   2500 calories
2.   175 grams protein
3.   69 grams fats
4.   294 grams carbs

Remember that this diet plan is only an example. You need to compute your own calorie maintenance level in order to know the appropriate measurement of protein, fat, carb, and calorie that you need to consume each day.

4) EATING TO BURN FAT AND GET SHREDDED

In the previous chapter, I detailed how you should be able to gain muscle. In this chapter, I will explain how to lose weight which is helpful if you need to lose fat before you start bodybuilding, or if you are looking to get shredded.

WHY PEOPLE CAN'T LOSE WEIGHT

1.   You will not lose weight if you consume excess calories. In order to lose weight, you have to burn more calories and eat less.
2.   A hormonal imbalance could be the culprit. Medical professionals discovered that an under-active thyroid can cause weight gain.
3.   Some medications may cause you to gain weight. If you are taking antihistamines or antidepressants, it can be difficult for you to lose weight. If you are currently on medication and you think it might be the reason why you can't lose weight, speak to your doctor about alternatives.
4.   You can't lose weight if you're relying solely on exercise.
5.   A slow metabolism can make it hard for you to lose weight.

HOW TO CALCULATE CALORIE INTAKE TO BURN FAT

If you want to lose weight, you should have a calorie deficit. This could be done by reducing consumption of food or by engaging in more physical activities. If your goal is to get shredded, you'll need an effective exercise routine.
This weight loss should be healthy; you should not starve yourself or speed up weight loss. You will still need to consume from the entire food groups so you will maintain proper body function and stay healthy.

If you want to lose fat, you will need to eat 20% below your CML.

You should aim to lose between ½ pound to 2 pounds per week and no more. The losses should be closer to 2 pounds if you are starting off at a high BMI, or you have a lot of weight to lose. If you are losing less than ½ pound, or are not losing any weight at all, you need to reduce your intake of calories by another 10%.

Note that someone who is obese, should eat less carbohydrates and fat in proportion to their total calories. Carbohydrates tend to play a big role in weight gain, so those who are looking to lose weight should go for higher portions of protein over carbs and fat.

Important points to remember when shredding:

1.   First, don't forget to maintain your protein intake. If your protein intake is low, chances are you'll also lose your muscle mass along the way.
2.   Try alternating between low carb and medium carb days.
3.   Lastly, drink about a gallon of water each day. Water can keep you healthy and hydrated.

Tracking Your Progress:

As previously stated, choose a common time every week to weigh yourself and keep a record of these weights so you can see how much your gaining/losing. This way you can adjust your diet accordingly. The most beneficial way of tracking progress is by looking in the mirror though! The scales and tape measures can only tell you so much.

SAMPLE MEAL PLAN

Nutrition Facts:
Protein – 40%
Fat – 30%
Carbohydrate – 30%
Calorie – 2,200

Breakfast (420 Calories)
0.5 large banana
250 ml skimmed milk
48 g peanut butter

Morning Snack (350 Calories)
1 apple
40 g almonds

Lunch (350 calories)
200 grams broccoli
200 grams carrots
10 grams almond
1 piece of chicken fillet

Pre-Workout Snack (330 Calories)
25 grams whey protein
1 apple
375 ml skimmed milk

Post-Workout Snack (350 Calories)
250 ml skimmed milk
2 50 grams whey protein
0.5 large banana

Dinner (380 calories)
200 grams green beans
1.5 salmon fillet
1 tablespoon olive oil

5) PRE & POST WORKOUT NUTRITION

Your body needs fuel in order to move. This is why pre-workout meals or drinks are very important.

- You need nutrients to boost your energy, depending on your workout activity.
- Eating the proper nutrients after your training will help your body improve in performance and recover quickly.

Protein synthesis is a crucial process in lean muscle building, and in fact, post workout meals focus primarily on making sure that it occurs. To those who have been lifting for a long time, protein synthesis peaks way earlier. Long-time bodybuilders and weight lifters experience it 4 hours after working out. If you are a complete beginner to muscle building, it might take around 6 hours, or even longer. According to a study conducted in 2013, the results of which were published in the Journal of the International Society of Sports Nutrition, muscles of the average person are most receptive to protein 4-6 hours after working out.

This is why protein intake before and after a rigorous workout is crucial. This means that you should have a protein-rich meal 2-3 hours before working out, and then another one 1-2 hours after training. You need protein to repair your tissues, and to get muscle growth going. Your body automatically reverts to 'repair mode' if these nutrients are readily available.

Protein synthesis slows down during sleep, so you should eat something as soon as you wake up if you're planning to train.

Sample Post Workout Meal

1.   Protein Pancake
Ingredients:
1/8 teaspoon baking powder
½ cup cottage cheese
½ teaspoon vanilla extract
½ cup oats
4 egg whites

How to make:

Mix all ingredients and cook as you would any pancakes. Once cooked, top the pancakes with berries or fresh banana slices.

2.   Crackers With Tuna
Ingredients:
½ cup of crushed crackers, whole grain
1 can of tuna, yellow fin

How to make:
Mix all ingredients and add pepper, pickles and mustard to taste.

3.   Oats
Ingredients:
½ cup almonds, dried or frozen
½ cup rolled oats
1 scoop whey protein

How to make:
Mix all ingredients and refrigerate overnight. Add cinnamon for added taste.

So, let's get started!

Now you know how many calories your should be eating, the recommended percentages of proteins, fats and carbs and have stocked up your kitchen - you're ready to go!

The rest of this book is dedicated to providing you with 300 recipes that you can use whether you're looking to build muscle or get shredded. They are easy to cook, taste delicious and won't get boring.

So get out of the rut of boiled chicken and raw eggs and try your hand at these delicious meals.

If your looking to shred, simply keep track of the calories you're consuming. All the meals have been created to be lean and fresh and so are suitable for bulking and shredding.

Apps like myfitnesspal can help you keep track of your calories and even show you the ratio of fats, carbs and proteins you have consumed. But I've included a breakdown of all the nutritional information for each dish to help you total it up and make your life easy.

If you need to adjust anything, simply adjust! Add extra proteins to recipes for higher protein count and reduce the carbohydrates you pair with the meals to lower carb content.

We wish you all the best on your bodybuilding journey - it always starts with the first step!

BREAKFAST

It's the most important meal of the day. Your parents told you. Your teachers told you. And now you know it. How can you expect not to have a total burn out, or beat your PB, or even have the energy to get your ass off the sofa if you haven't fuelled the machine? You can't. So use these quick, easy and tasty recipes to get you going. And no, it's not all raw eggs…

MASS BUILDING SWEET POTATO PANCAKES

Start your day with this quick and easy, delicious protein packed pancake recipe. It contains all the right ingredients to keep you going and more than enough protein for your muscles to feast on!

Ingredients

1 medium sized sweet potato
1 egg
4 egg whites
8oz fat-free Greek yogurt
1/2 cup of oats
1 tsp cinnamon
1 tsp vanilla extract
1 tsp of honey
Handful of diced strawberries
Handful of blueberries

How to make:

1. Rinse sweet potato under cold water for a couple of seconds and then pierce it with a fork several times and place it in the microwave until soft (about 8 minutes).
2. After let it cool down before removing all skin with a knife.
3. Put the oats into a blender and blend until they are a fine powder, then place into a bowl.
4. Place the sweet potato in the blender and blend until smooth, and then mix with the powdered oats.
5. Add the egg, egg whites, vanilla, cinnamon, honey and yogurt and stir well. This is now your pancake batter.
6. Spray a pan with cooking spray and place over medium heat. Pour roughly a quarter of the batter into the pan and cook for 1-2 minutes. Flip the pancake and cook for another 30 seconds
7. Once done, remove your tasty pancake and top with the berries. 7. Use the same method for the rest of your batter.

Calories per serving: 451, Protein: 38g Carbs: 74g, Fat: 9g

BRAWNY BREAKFAST BURRITO

Add a bit spice to your life with this Mexican inspired burrito. Contains great sources of protein, healthy fats and fibre to ensure you're building muscle the lean way.

Ingredients

2 eggs
1/2 cup of low fat milk
1/4 cup of black beans
4oz of low fat cheese
Handful of chopped red peppers
1 tsp of chopped coriander
1 tbsp of salsa
½ tsp of cumin

How to make:

1. Add the milk, eggs and cumin to a bowl and whisk together.
2. Spray pan with cooking spray and place over medium heat. Add the mixture to the pan. After roughly 2 – 3 minutes, add the low fat cheese, chopped red peppers and black beans to the omelette.
3. Once added fold the omelette in half and let it

cook through (1-2 minutes).

4. Remove from pan and serve with the salsa and coriander.

Calories per serving: 302, Protein: 25g Carbs: 19g, Fat: 16g

SUPER SCRAMBLED TURKEY BACON EGGS ON TOAST

Mix up your boring egg based breakfasts with this delicious recipe. Eggs are a great source of complete protein as they contain all eight amino acids.

Ingredients

6 egg whites
3 slices of turkey bacon
2 slices of Ezekiel or wholemeal bread
Handful of chopped onion
Handful of chopped yellow peppers
Handful of chopped white mushrooms
1 tsp of garlic powder
1 tsp of dried parsley
1 tsp of olive oil

How to make:

1. Spray pan with cooking spray and place over medium/high heat. Add the chopped onions, chopped yellow peppers and white mushrooms and cook until soft.
2. In a different pan, cook the turkey bacon.
3. Add the egg whites and garlic powder to the pan with the veggies and 1tsp of olive oil and scramble until the eggs become firm.
4. Toast the Ezekiel bread.
5. Break up the turkey bacon and add to the scrambled eggs
6. Plate up and serve scrambled eggs and turkey

bacon on bread, sprinkled with the fresh parsley.

7. Add salt and pepper as required.

Calories per serving: 299, Protein: 22g Carbs: 35g, Fat: 8g

BANANA AND ALMOND MUSCLE OATMEAL

If you're in a hurry, this recipe is great. It takes around 5 minutes to make and still has the right macronutrients to make this a healthy and sustaining meal.

Ingredients

1/2 cup of rolled oats
1 cup of low fat milk
1 scoop of whey protein (vanilla or chocolate)
Handful of chopped almonds
1 tsp of organic peanut butter
1 diced banana

How to make:

1. Throw the oats and low fat milk into a large bowl, stir and place in the microwave for two minutes.
2. Add the diced banana, peanut butter, whey protein and chopped almonds to the oats and mix in.

(Serves 1)

Calories per serving: 523, Protein: 32g Carbs: 16g, Fat: 15g

PROTEIN POWERED PANCAKES

If you're not a fan of sweet potato, then these are a great alternative. Lots of protein and quick and easy to make.

Ingredients

6 egg whites
1/2 cup of rolled oats
1 tsp flaxseed oil
1 tsp of cinnamon
1 tsp of stevia

How to make:

1. Put the oats and all the other ingredients into a blender and blend. This is now your pancake batter.
2. Spray pan with cooking spray and place over medium heat.
3. Pour roughly 1/5 of the pancake batter into the pan and cook for 1-2 minutes. Flip the pancake and cook for another 30 seconds.
4. Once done, remove your tasty pancake.
5. Use the same method for the rest of your batter.

Serves 2 (Makes about 5 pancakes)

Calories per serving: 337, Protein: 27g, Carbs: 33g, Fat: 9g

TURKEY MUSCLE OMELETTE

If you're looking for a protein packed, low carb meal for breakfast then this is it. Contains 26 grams of protein and only 5 grams of carbs.

Ingredients

10oz of chopped or minced turkey
3 eggs
Handful of baby spinach
Handful of kale
1 tbsp of olive oil
1/4 cup of low fat cheese

How to make:

1. Crack the eggs into a bowl and whisk.
2. Grab a pan and heat half the oil on a medium heat, then add the turkey, kale and cheese and cook for 5-6 minutes.
3. In a different pan, heat the rest of the olive oil and then add the eggs and cook for around 4 minutes.
4. Add the turkey mix into the pan with the eggs and sprinkle some baby spinach on top, then fold the omelette in half.
5. Cook for another 2-3 minutes.
6. Plate up and serve.

(Serves 2)

Calories per serving: 358, Protein: 26g, Carbs: 5g, Fat: 21g

AESTHETIC ASPARAGUS FRITTATA

A high protein and low carb breakfast which is great for those who are looking to minimize their carb intake.

Ingredients

2 cups of chopped asparagus
½ broccoli (florets only)
8 eggs
Handful of chopped parsley
1 tsp of chives
1 tbsp of olive oil
1 cup of low fat milk
Salt and pepper

How to make:

1. Crack the eggs into a bowl, add the milk and some salt and pepper and whisk.
2. Get a covered skillet and steam the broccoli over a medium heat for 4-5 minutes. Set to one side.
3. Next, in the same skillet, heat the oil. Add the chopped asparagus, chopped parsley and chives into the skillet and cook for around 2-3 minutes on a medium heat.
4. Add the egg mixture, along with the broccoli into the skillet and cover the skillet evenly.
5. Cook for around 3-4 minutes or until the eggs are set right through
6. Take the skillet and place under the grill for around 2 minutes or until the top is golden (optional).
7. Plate up and serve.

(Serves 3)

Calories per serving: 349, Protein: 23g ,Carbs: 8g, Fat: 25g

POWER PROTEIN WAFFLES

Who said waffles are unhealthy? My waffle recipes are packed full of protein and without the guilt on the side!

Ingredients

4 eggs whites
1 scoop of vanilla protein powder
1/2 cup of rolled oats
1 tsp of baking powder
½ tsp of stevia

How to make:

1. Add all the ingredients into a blender and blend.
2. Add the mixture to a waffle iron and bake.

Calories per serving: 314, Protein: 37g, Carbs: 28g, Fat: 5g

SCRAMBLED EGGS WITH SPINACH

Tasty, quick and easy breakfast packed full of protein

Ingredients

3 eggs
5 egg whites
1 cup of baby spinach
1/2 cup of grated low fat cheese
Handful of chopped onion
Handful of chopped red peppers
1 tsp of olive oil

How to make:

1. Spray pan with cooking spray and place over medium/high heat.
2. Add the chopped onions, chopped red peppers and cook until soft.
3. Add the egg and egg whites to the pan with the veggies with 1tsp of olive oil and scramble until the eggs become firm.
4. Sprinkle the baby spinach leaves and cheese over the eggs.
5. Plate up and serve scrambled eggs.
6. Add salt and pepper as required.

(Serves 2)

Calories per serving: 282, Protein: 23g, Carbs: 15g, Fat: 15g

MIGHTY QUINOA BREAKFAST CEREAL

Start your protein kick early in the morning without having to down the raw eggs!

Ingredients

1 1/2 Cup quinoa
1 Cup blackberries
3 Cup water
1/4 Tsp ground nutmeg
1/2 Tsp vanilla extract

How to make:

1. Get a pan and combine all of the ingredients, cooking over medium to high heat until boiling.
2. Once boiling, cover and simmer for 15 minutes or until the quinoa is soft and the liquid has been absorbed.
3. Pour into serving bowls and enjoy.

(Serves 2)

Calories per serving: 527, Protein: 22g, Carbs: 96g, Fat: 9g

BOUNTY OATS

Start your day right with coconut and choco-latey oats.

Ingredients

2 Cups wholemeal oats
1 Tbsp milled chia seeds
3 Cups coconut milk
1 Scoop chocolate protein powder
1 Tbsp coconut shavings
6 Strawberries (or any fruit of your choice)

How to make:

1. In a pan mix the oats, and coconut milk.
2. Heat on a medium heat and then simmer until the oats are fully cooked through (5-10 minutes).
3. Pour into your favorite breakfast bowl and stir in the protein powder, strawberries and milled chia seeds on top.
4. If you've got a sweet tooth or fancy an extra treat, try adding cacao or a drizzle of honey to serve.

(Serves 2)

Calories per serving: 550, Protein: 22g, Carbs: 63g, Fat: 24g

BRAWNY FRUIT & NUT GRANOLA

Homemade power cereal!

Ingredients

1 Cup wholemeal or steel cut oats
1/3 Cup buckwheat
2 Cups water
1/3 Cup sunflower seeds
1/3 Cup pumpkin seeds
1/2 Cup almonds
1/3 Cup blueberries
1/2 Cup of peeled and finely chopped apples
1 Tbsp coconut oil
1 Tsp ginger (fresh and grated)

How to make:

1. Preheat the oven to 350°f/180°c/Gas Mark 4.
2. Meanwhile mix the oats, buckwheat, nuts and seeds into a bowl.
3. Put the berries, apples, coconut oil and water to cover in a pan; cover and simmer for 10-15 minutes on a medium-high heat until the fruits are soft to touch. Then stir in the ginger.
4. Add the fruit mixture to a blender until smooth.
5. Mix the fruits with the buckwheat.
6. Grease a baking tray with coconut oil and then spread the granola mixture on top using a knife or spatula to create a thin layer. Bake for 45 minutes.
7. Stir the mixture every 15 minutes so it doesn't burn. When crispy all over, remove the tray and allow to cool.
8. Serve as a crispy breakfast treat alongside low fat yogurt and fresh fruit if desired.

(Serves 4)

Calories per serving: 665, Protein: 22g, Carbs: 77g, Fat: 36g

SIZZLING SAUSAGE PATTIES

These patties are made with lean ground pork and no added preservatives! Enjoy.

Ingredients

18oz of lean ground pork
2 Tsp fresh chopped sage leaves
1 Tsp chopped thyme
1 Tsp ground black pepper
1/4 Tsp ground nutmeg
1/4 Tsp cayenne pepper
1/4 Tsp chopped oregano
1 Tbsp extra virgin olive oil
4 eggs

How to make:

1. Get a mixing bowl and add all of the ingredients.
2. Mix with a spoon or blender until blended and form 8 patties using the palms of your hands to shape.
3. Heat the oil in a skillet, over a medium heat and cook the patties for 9 minutes one side and 9 on the other side until they're browned and cooked through.

(Serves 4)

Calories per serving: 440, Protein: 17g, Carbs: 31g, Fat: 29g

GET-FIT FRITTATA

Great for a quick breakfast at home or in a Tupperware for after training!

Ingredients

1 Tbsp coconut or extra virgin olive oil
4 Eggs
1 Sweet potato, peeled and sliced
1 Peeled and sliced red bell pepper
2 Tsp oregano
1/2 Peeled and sliced zucchini
1 Tsp cracked black pepper
1 Cup spinach leaves/arugula

How to make:

1. Preheat broiler on a medium heat.
2. Heat the oil in a skillet under the broiler until hot.
3. Spread the potato slices across the skillet and cooking for 8-10 minutes or until soft.
4. Add the zucchini and red bell pepper to the skillet and cook for a further 5 minutes.
5. Meanwhile, whisk the eggs and oregano in a separate bowl, and season to taste before pouring mixture over the veggies in the skillet.
6. Cook for 10 minutes on a low heat until golden.
7. Remove and turn over onto a plate or serving board.
8. Serve with a side of spinach leaves or arugula.
9. Cut the frittata into slices to serve.

(Serves 2)

Calories per serving: 337, Protein: 17g, Carbs: 33g, Fat: 15g

EGGS IN AVOCADOS!

Poach the egg and float it in its own avocado boat; full of healthy fats and protein to start your day.

Ingredients

2 ripe avocado
4 eggs
1 tbsp white wine vinegar

How to make:

1. Place a large pan of water on a high heat and boil.
2. Once boiling add white wine vinegar (don't worry if you don't have it, it just helps with the poaching).
3. Lower the heat to a simmer and crack the eggs in. Top tip: do it quickly and from a height to get a nice round shape.
4. Stir the water ever now and then around the eggs to keep them moving and cook for 2 minutes for a very runny yolk; 2-4 minutes for a soft to firm yolk and 5 for a hard yolk.
5. Whilst cooking, prepare your avocado by cutting through to the stone lengthways around the whole of the fruit.
6. Use your palms on each side to twist the avocado and it should come away into 2 halves. Using your knife, carefully wedge it into the stone and pull to remove the stone. Alternatively, cut around the stone with the knife and use the sharp end to coax it out.
7. Use your avocado halves as a dish for the eggs and serve.
8. Season to taste! Yum.

(Serves 2)

Calories per serving: 334, Protein: 14g, Carbs: 18g, Fat: 37g

BRILLIANT BREAKFAST BIRCHER

Greek yogurt is high in protein and a staple bodybuilding ingredient! Tastes great for breakfast or as a snack.

Ingredients

1 Cup of wholegrain oats
2 Tangerines, peeled and sliced
1/2 Cup pineapple, chopped
16 Oz. Low fat greek yogurt
1 Tbsp coconut shavings

How to make:

1. Mix the oats and fruit with the yogurt and allow to soak for as long as possible (overnight is best).
2. Serve and top with coconut shavings – the oats should be nice and mushy and will have soaked up the flavors of the fruit.

(Serves 2)

Calories per serving: 395, Protein: 28g, Carbs: 52g, Fat: 10g

MIGHTY MINI MEATLOAVES

Scrumptious, meaty treats.

Ingredients

1 Cup lean ground turkey
1 Cup skinless ground chicken
1/2 Cup coconut milk
1 Minced garlic clove
1/4 Cup parsley
1 Tbsp paprika
Sprinkle of black pepper
1 Tsp coconut oil

How to make:

1. Preheat the oven to 400°f/200°c/Gas Mark 6.
2. Mix turkey, chicken, garlic, parsley, paprika, and coconut milk together, mixing until the ingredients hold.
3. Season with black pepper to taste.
4. Line a muffin tin with coconut oil and divide the mixture into each hole.
5. Bake in the oven for 30 minutes or until the meat is cooked through.
6. Serve hot!

(Serves 2)

Calories per serving: 459, Protein: 53g, Carbs: 2g, Fat: 29g

SCORE-BOARD SCOTCH EGGS

A great addition to meal prep day - just pop in your containers for a breakfast treat or post-workout fuel!

Ingredients

16 Oz lean ground chicken
1/2 Tsp black pepper
1/2 Tsp cayenne pepper
1/2 Tsp paprika
1/2 Tsp cloves
1/2 Cup fresh parsley, finely chopped
1/2 Tbsp dried chives
1 Clove garlic, finely chopped
4 Free range eggs, boiled and peeled

How to make:

1. Preheat the oven to 375°F/190°C/Gas Mark 5.
2. Cover a baking sheet with parchment paper.
3. Combine the chicken with the paprika, cayenne pepper, pepper, cloves, chives, parsley and garlic in a mixing bowl and mix with your hands until thoroughly mixed.
4. Divide the mixture into 4 circular shapes with the palms of your hands.
5. Flatten each one into a pancake shape using the backs of your hands or a rolling pin.
6. Wrap the meat pancake around 1 egg, until it's covered. (You can moisten the meat with water first to help prevent it from sticking to your hands).
7. Bake in the oven for 25 minutes or until brown and crisp – check the meat is cooked through with a knife before serving.

(Serves 2)

Calories per serving: 424, Protein: 47g, Carbs: 4g, Fat: 22g

EPIC EGG MUFFINS

Energizing and delicious!

Ingredients

8oz cooked skinless chicken
1/3 Cup red onion, diced
1/3 Cup green bell pepper, diced
1/3 Cup bell pepper, diced
1 Tsp dried tarragon
6 Large eggs

How to make:

1. Line a muffin pan with 6 wrappers.
2. Mix vegetables together in a separate bowl.
3. Next, spoon the vegetable mixture and chicken pieces into the muffin trays up to about 2/3 full, allowing room for the eggs.
4. Beat the eggs with the thyme in a separate bowl or jug.
5. Pour beaten eggs into each muffin tray - leave 1cm gap at the top.
6. Place the muffin tray in the oven and bake for approximately 25 minutes or until eggs are cooked through.
7. Remove egg muffins and serve.

(Serves 3)

Calories per serving: 232, Protein: 31g, Carbs: 6g, Fat: 10g

TURKEY BACON OMELETTE

Protein rich and easy to prepare.

Ingredients

1 Tbsp extra virgin olive oil
1/2 Leek, diced
8 Oz turkey bacon
1 Green onion, diced
2 Tbsp water
Pinch of black pepper
2 Large egg whites
2 Large eggs

How to make:

1. Heat olive oil in a skillet over a medium to high heat.
2. Sauté the vegetables and turkey bacon for 4-5 minutes.
3. Using a whisk, mix together the egg, egg whites, pepper and water together in a separate bowl.
4. Pour the eggs into the skillet over the vegetables and cook for 5-6 minutes until the edges begin to set.
5. Use a spatula to gently lift the edges of the omelette and turn over in the pan.
6. Fold the omelette in half and continue cooking for 3-4 minutes.
7. Remove omelette from the pan and cut in half to serve.

(Serves 2)

Calories per serving: 236, Protein: 15g, Carbs: 6g, Fat: 15g

BANANA & HAZELNUT PERFECT PANCAKES OATMEAL

Fuel up with these spiced pancakes!

Wholesome and tasty!

Ingredients

6 Egg whites
1/2 Cup of rolled oats
1 Tsp flaxseed oil
1 Tsp of cinnamon
1 Tsp of stevia
1/2 Cup mixed berries
1/2 Cup greek yogurt

Ingredients

1 Cup wholegrain oats
2 Cups almond milk
2 Scoop vanilla protein powder
2 Bananas, chopped
1/4 Cup chopped hazelnuts

How to make:

1. Add the oats and milk into a large bowl, stir and place in the microwave for two minutes.
2. Add the banana, whey protein and chopped hazelnuts to the oats and stir well.
3. Serve warm.

(Serves 2)

Calories per serving: 532, Protein: 27g, Carbs: 53g, Fat: 17g

How to make:

1. Blend all ingredients in a food processor until smooth.
2. Spray a pan or skillet with cooking spray and heat over a medium heat.
3. Pour roughly 1/2 of the pancake batter into the pan and cook for 1-2 minutes. Flip the pancake and cook for another 30 seconds.
4. Once done, remove your tasty pancake.
5. Use the same method for the rest of your batter.
6. Serve with extra fruit of your choice.

(Serves 2)

Calories per serving: 262, Protein: 19g, Carbs: 27g, Fat: 9g

WORKOUT WAFFLES

You can still enjoy waffles whilst training with this recipe.

Ingredients

4 Egg whites
1 Scoop of chocolate protein powder
1/2 Cup of rolled oats
1 Tsp of baking powder
½ Tsp of stevia
1/2 Cup strawberries to serve

How to make:

1. Add all the ingredients into a blender and blend.
2. Add the mixture to a waffle iron and bake for 10 minutes.
3. Serve with fresh strawberries and enjoy!

(Serves 2)

Calories per serving: 270, Protein: 35g, Carbs: 23g, Fat: 4g

STRENGTHENING SPINACH SCRAMBLE

Healthy fats and protein combine in this tasty and fast breakfast.

Ingredients

2 Eggs
2 Egg Whites
1 Tsp Oregano
1 Tsp Parsley
1 Tsp Sesame Seeds
1 Cup Of Baby Spinach
4Oz Turkey Pieces, Cooked
1/2 Chopped Onion
1 Garlic Clove, Diced
1 Tsp Of Olive Oil
1 Avocado

How to make:

1. Add oil to a skillet and place over a medium to high heat.
2. Add the chopped onion and garlic and cook for 5 minutes or until soft.
3. Add the turkey pieces and continue to cook for 3-4 minutes.
4. Whisk the eggs and egg whites in a separate bowl and add oregano and parsley.
5. Add the eggs to the pan and stir through.
6. Continue to stir for 5-6 minutes or until eggs are cooked through.
7. Add the spinach to the pan and stir through for 2-3 minutes or until wilted.
8. Peel and slice the avocado and serve on the side of the scrambled eggs.
9. Sprinkle with the sesame seeds and a little black pepper.
10. Enjoy!

(Serves 2)

Calories per serving: 411, Protein: 30g, Carbs: 13g, Fat: 35g

SWEET POTATO PANCAKES

Sweet and savoury pancakes - the sweet potatoes will keep you going for longer.

Ingredients

1 Sweet potato
1 Tsp olive oil
1 Egg
4 Egg whites
1 Cup fat-free greek yogurt
1/2 Cup oats
1 Tsp maple syrup
1 Banana, sliced

How to make:

1. Rinse sweet potato and add to a microwaveable sandwich bag with olive oil.
2. Microwave for 12 minutes.
3. Remove and allow to cool before removing the skin from the sweet potato with a sharp knife.
4. If you don't have a microwave, simply pierce sweet potato with a fork and add to a hot oven for 20-30 minutes or until soft.
5. Put the oats into a blender and blend to a fine powder, then place into a bowl.
6. Place the sweet potato in the blender and blend until smooth, and then mix with the powdered oats.

7. Add the egg, egg whites, maple syrup and yogurt and stir well.
8. Spray a pan with cooking spray and place over a medium heat.
9. Pour roughly a quarter of the batter into the pan and cook for 1-2 minutes.
10. Flip the pancake and cook for another 30 seconds.
11. Enjoy hot with sliced banana to serve (optional).
12. Use the same method for the rest of your batter.

(Serves 2)

Calories per serving: 376, Protein: 16g, Carbs: 45g, Fat: 15g

CLASSIC STEAK, MUSHROOM & EGGS

It's a cliché for a reason!

Ingredients

2X 6oz of rump beef steaks
1 Tsp paprika
1 Tsp mixed dried herbs
2 Eggs
1 Large beef tomato, sliced in half

I large field mushroom, sliced in half

How to make:

1. Heat the broiler on high.
2. Sprinkle paprika and herbs over each side of the steaks.
3. Add the steaks to a baking tray/griddle pan and place under the broiler.
4. Cook using the following approximate timings for each side:

5. 2 minutes = rare
6. 3-4 minutes = medium
7. 5-6 minutes = well done
8. Whilst the steak is cooking, add the tomato and mushroom to the pan, turning once through cooking.
9. Remove the steak and vegetables from the pan once done and allow to rest.
10. Crack the eggs onto the pan/tray and allow to cook for 4-5 minutes or until cooked through (3-4 minutes for a runny yolk and add a couple of minutes for a hard yolk).
11. Plate up and serve!

(Serves 2)

Calories per serving: 470, Protein: 60g, Carbs: 6g, Fat: 23g

PUMPIN' PUMPKIN PANCAKES

Savoury , tasty and healthy pancakes.

Ingredients

Flesh from 1/4 deseeded pumpkin
2 Tbsp water
4 Eggs
3 Egg whites
1 Tsp of black pepper
1 Tsp gluten-free baking soda
2 Tbsp coconut oil
1 Tbsp raw honey
1 Handful walnuts

How to make:

1. In a blender or food processor, blend the pumpkin flesh together with water to form a smooth pulp.
2. Now add the eggs, freshly ground pepper, 1 tbsp of coconut oil, and baking soda to the pumpkin mix and blend until smooth.
3. Heat a large pan on a medium heat with the 1 tbsp of coconut oil.
4. Pour into the pan into individual rounded pancakes.
5. Lift the mixture with a spatula and then flip.
6. Cook for 3 minutes on either side.
7. Plate and serve with walnuts and honey.
8. Plate up and serve!

(Serves 2)

Calories per serving: 435, Protein: 21g, Carbs: 14g, Fat: 33g

BODYBUILDER'S BANANA PANCAKES

Get 1 of your 5 a day with these tasty pancakes.

Ingredients

2 Scoops Unflavored Protein Powder
1/2 Cup Whole Grain Flour
1/4 Cup Rolled Oats
1 Banana, Mashed
1 Large Egg
1 Tbsp Almond Milk
1 Tsp Raw Honey
1 Cup Strawberries

How to make:

1. Thoroughly mix the protein powder, flour and oats in a large bowl.
2. Add the banana, egg and almond milk and mix in well.
3. Add frying spray to a non-stick skillet and heat over a medium heat.
4. Pour 1/4 batter into the pan and allow to sit for 2-3 minutes before flipping.
5. Repeat for the rest of the batter and serve 2 pancakes each with honey and strawberries on top.

(Serves 2)

Calories per serving: 400, Protein: 28g, Carbs: 55g, Fat: 7g

CHERRY PROTEIN PORRIDGE

Warm & sweet!

Ingredients

2 Cups rolled oats
1/2 Cup cherries
2 Scoops vanilla protein powder
4 Cups almond milk

How to make:

1. Mix the oats with the almond milk in a large bowl.
2. Add to a pan on the stove over a medium heat until it starts to bubble slightly but not boil.
3. Alternatively place in the microwave for 1.5 minutes.
4. Remove from the pan and return to the large bowl.
5. Stir in the protein powder until there are no lumps left.
6. Top with cherries and serve.

(Serves 2)

Calories per serving: 370, Protein: 27g, Carbs: 41g, Fat: 11g

MUSCLE FRUIT & NUT PROTEIN CEREAL

Some vegetarians are deficient in omega 3 fatty acids that are sourced primarily from fish. This recipe will address that problem and provide all the benefits from healthy fat

Ingredients

2 tbsp of dried apricots
1 scoop of vanilla protein powder
1 tbsp of flaked almonds
1 tbsp of dried raisins
1 tbsp of Chia seeds
1 tbsp of buckwheat
1 tbsp of hemp seeds
1 tbsp of dried cranberries
3/4 cup of cashew milk

How to make:

1. Get a small bowl and combine all of the dry ingredients.
2. Pour the cashew milk on top. Serve immediately.

(Serves 1)

Calories per serving: 450, Protein: 18g ,Carbs: 55g, Fat: 21g

LEAN & MEAN VEGGIE BURGER

This is the perfect on-the-go meal for the busy bodybuilder.

Ingredients

2 regular-sized eggs
Handful of baby spinach leaves
1 whole wheat roll
1 veggie burger patty

How to make:

1. Fry the veggie burger patty in a pan on a medium heat for 7-10 minutes.
2. Fry the egg in the same pan for 3-4 minutes.
3. Prepare the roll with the egg and spinach topping the burger.
4. Serve and enjoy.

(Serves 1)

Calories per serving: 441, Protein: 27g ,Carbs: 16g, Fat: 14g

COCONUT POWERED PANCAKES

Providing a new twist to the traditional home-cooked breakfast favourite, this recipe is light on the tummy but packs enough protein for muscle building.

Ingredients

4 egg whites
2 tbsp of coconut flour
1 tsp of cinnamon
1 scoop of vanilla protein powder
1 diced regular-sized banana
Handful of walnuts
Handful of almonds
1 dash of cinnamon
2 tbsp honey

How to make:

1. Pre-heat a skillet over medium to high heat.
2. Blend all the ingredients together. Pour roughly ½ cup of the pancake batter into the pan and cook for 1-2 minutes. Flip the pancake and cook for another 30 seconds. Once done, remove your tasty pancake. Use the same method for the rest of your batter.
3. Serve and enjoy immediately.

(Serves 2)

Calories per serving: 323, Protein: 22g ,Carbs: 25g, Fat: 15g

RIPPED & READY PANCAKES

Even without slathering your plate with sweet syrup, these pancakes are already tasty and sweet as they are!.

Ingredients

2oz gluten free flour
4 egg whites
1/2 tsp of baking powder
1 tbsp of blueberries
1 tbsp of walnuts

How to make:

1. Pre-heat a skillet over medium to high heat.
2. Blend all the ingredients together. Pour roughly ½ cup of the pancake batter into the pan and cook for 1-2 minutes. Flip the pancake and cook for another 30 seconds. Once done, remove your tasty pancake. Use the same method for the rest of your batter.
3. Serve and enjoy immediately.

(Serves 1)

Calories per serving: 315, Protein: 19g ,Carbs: 35g, Fat: 11g

BRAWNY APPLE, KALE & BLUEBERRY SMOOTHIE

If you love having a fruit smoothie for breakfast, why not add some kale to your drink and spike up your breakfast with plenty of health benefits? Quick and easy to prepare, you won't even taste the veggies in your drink.

Ingredients

1/2 cup of kale
1 chopped and halved apple
1/2 cup of frozen blueberries
1 scoop of vanilla protein powder
1/2 tbsp of unsweetened almond milk
1 to 2 ice cubes

How to make:

1. Combine all the ingredients together in a blender and process until smooth consistency is achieved.
2. Serve immediately and enjoy

(Serves 1)

Calories per serving: 312, Protein: 27g ,Carbs: 42g, Fat: 4g

OAT MUSCLE MUSH

Mush for breakfast? Why Not? As long as you get the nutrients you need to jumpstart your day, there should be no problem – and this gives a boost and more!

Ingredients

1 cup of oatmeal
4 egg whites
1 tsp of honey
2 tbsp of unsweetened almond milk
1/2 scoop of Chocolate protein powder
4 diced strawberries
1 tbsp of almond butter

How to make:

1. Get a small bowl and combine all the ingredients.
2. Heat in the microwave oven for 1 or 2 minutes, or until the oats have absorbed all the liquid.
3. Add the strawberries and almond butter to the top.
4. Serve and enjoy.

(Serves 1)

Calories per serving: 536, Protein: 33g ,Carbs: 74g, Fat: 14g

BRAWNY VEGGIE SAUSAGE CLUB

Who says vegetarians miss out on home-made breakfast classics like this? With a little creativity, vegetarians don't have to miss anything – except the meat!

Ingredients

2 large veggie sausage patties
2 large eggs
1 slice of whole grain bread
1/2 cup spinach leaves

How to make:

1. Bring a pan of water to the boil and add a dash of white wine vinegar and salt. Reduce the heat and crack the eggs in, allowing to float as it is in the water. Cook for 3 minutes (check that the whites are opaque).
2. While the eggs are cooking, heat a frying pan with some vegetable oil and lightly fry the veggie patties until heated through.
3. Toss in the spinach to wilt at the last minute.
4. Serve with the toasted wholegrain bread.

(Serves 1)

Calories per serving: 472, Protein: 42g ,Carbs: 32g, Fat: 21g

POACHED EGGS WITH SUPER SPINACH & KALE

You could expect to be served this dish in any top restaurant; poached eggs make anything posh and they're also probably the healthiest way of cooking your eggs to make the most of all that protein.

Ingredients

4 medium-sized eggs
1/2 cup kale (stems removed)
1/2 cup baby spinach
1 tbsp of olive oil
1 tbsp of white wine vinegar
1 crushed and finely chopped garlic clove
Sprinkle of salt
Sprinkle of pepper

How to make:

1. Heat olive oil in a skillet on a medium heat and add the garlic.
2. Toss in kale and sauté until wilted or for about 2 to 3 minutes. Transfer the kale onto a plate and set aside.
3. Boil water in a large pot. Once it boils, reduce the heat and add 1 tbsp of white wine vinegar.
4. Crack the eggs in and allow to cook until for about 3 minutes or when the egg whites are not translucent anymore.
5. Remove the eggs and lay on top of the kale and baby spinach.
6. Sprinkle with a dash of salt & pepper to taste.
7. Serve and enjoy while hot.

(Serves 2)

Calories per serving: 170, Protein: 15g , Carbs: 5g, Fat: 10g

CHICKEN AND POULTRY

Chicken breast and eggs: the first things that come to mind when you think about what meals you will have to subject yourself to for breakfast, lunch and dinner for the rest of your muscle-building life. But there is so much more out there within the chicken and poultry meal options. We all know chicken is great – it's low in fat and high in protein and it's tasty, so read on and find out how chicken and other poultry members can be exciting and effective in your meal-plan diary.

QUICK AND EASY GRILLED CHICKEN WRAPS

These are quick to prepare and full of protein to build muscle and burn fat. Ideal for lunch-boxes!

Ingredients

2 whole-wheat tortilla wraps
4oz of chopped grilled chicken
1 tsp of low-fat mayonnaise
Handful of baby spinach leaves
1/2 a sliced cucumber
1/2 chopped red pepper

How to make:

1. Get 1 whole-wheat tortilla and spread the low-fat mayonnaise across the centre.
2. Add the grilled chicken, cucumber, spinach leaves and red pepper to the mayonnaise and roll the tortilla up.
3. Repeat the process with the last tortilla.

(Serves 1)

Calories per serving: 437, Protein: 48g, Carbs: 39g, Fat: 10g

ANABOLIC JERK CHICKEN AND BROWN RICE

Add a little spice to your life with this traditional Caribbean dish. Packed full of protein and slow releasing carbohydrates to keep to you growing!

Ingredients

4oz of chicken thighs or breast
½ tsp of ground allspice
½ tsp of black pepper
½ tsp of nutmeg
½ tsp of cinnamon
½ tsp of sage
½ tsp of dried thyme
1 clove of garlic
½ tsp of dried thyme
1 chopped onion
2 chopped and deseeded scotch bonnet chillies
1/2 chopped red pepper
1/2 cup of brown rice
1 tsp of olive oil

How to make:

1. To make the jerk paste, add the allspice, nutmeg, sage, cinnamon, dried thyme, garlic, red pepper, black pepper, onion, olive oil and scotch bonnet chillies to the blender and blend until it's a puree.
2. Rub the paste over the chicken breasts and leave them for at least one hour to marinade.
3. Add the chicken breasts to the grill and grill them for roughly 10-12 minutes per side or until they are cooked through. Put to one side once cooked.
4. Meanwhile add 300ml of cold water to a pot and heat until the water is boiling. Once boiling, add the rice and leave for 20 minutes.

5. Drain the rice and serve with the chicken.

(Serves 1)

Calories per serving: 516, Protein: 32g, Carbs: 76g, Fat: 33g

LAZY CHICKEN AND EGG STIR FRY

This meal is quick to prepare and contains two great protein sources to build muscle and burn fat.

Ingredients

4oz of chopped chicken breast
2 eggs
1 cup of brown rice
2 tsp of chinese five spice
1 cup of mixed frozen veg

How to make:

1. Add 300ml of cold water to a pot and heat until the water is boiling. Once boiling, add the rice and leave for 20 minutes. Drain the rice and place to one side.
2. Heat a pan on a medium heat and add the chopped chicken and spices.
3. Stir-fry for roughly 5 minutes.
4. While the chicken is cooking, boil or steam the frozen veg for 5 minutes until cooked and beat the eggs in a separate bowl.
5. Add the rice and beaten eggs to the pan with the chicken and stir until the eggs start to scramble 3-4 minutes.
6. Finally add the veg to the pan and stir for a further 2-3 minutes

(Serves 1)

Calories per serving: 409, Protein: 46g, Carbs: 89g, Fat: 20g

POWER PESTO CHICKEN PASTA

Great protein packed pasta dish to mix things up!

Ingredients

8oz of chopped grilled chicken breast
1 cup of whole-wheat pasta
1 tbsp of pesto
A pinch of black pepper
Handful of basil
Handful of spinach
Handful of rocket
Handful of pine nuts
Handful of diced tomatoes
2 tbsp of olive oil

How to make:

1. Heat a large pan of water on high until it boils.
2. Add the whole-wheat pasta and leave until the water returns to boiling point.
3. Reduce the heat until the water simmers. Leave the whole-wheat pasta to cook for around 10 minutes.
4. Get a bowl and add the pesto, olive oil and black pepper and mix together.
5. Add the chopped chicken breast, pine nuts, tomatoes and herbs to the mixture.
6. Drain the pasta and fold the mix into the pan until the pasta is covered.

(Serves 2)

Calories per serving: 550, Protein: 25g, Carbs: 30g, Fat: 19g

MUSCLE MOROCCAN CHICKEN CASSEROLE

A classic Moroccan casserole packed with lots of protein, high in flavour and also very low in fat.

Ingredients

4 chicken breasts
1 tsp of ground cumin
1 tsp of paprika
1 tbsp of olive oil
1 chopped onion
12oz of canned chopped tomatoes
2 tbsp harissa paste
1 tbsp honey
2 medium thickly sliced courgettes
14oz of drained and rinsed chickpeas
A pinch of salt and pepper

How to make:

1. Sprinkle salt, pepper, paprika and the ground cumin over the chicken breasts.
2. Then grab a large pan and add the olive oil and heat on a medium heat.
3. Add the chicken and onions to the pan and cook the chicken for roughly four minutes per side.
4. Pour the chopped tomatoes into the pan along with 1/2 cup of water and add the honey, harissa, courgettes and chickpeas and stir the ingredients together.
5. Bring the mix to a simmer and then leave to cook for around 15 minutes.
6. Plate up and serve.

(Serves 4)

Calories per serving: 404, Protein: 47g, Carbs: 37g, Fat: 8g

BRAWNY CHICKEN & CHORIZO JAMBALAYA

A very tasty muscle-building recipe, inspired by Cajun cuisine. Contains a good helping of protein and slow releasing carbs to keep you burning fat and building muscle.

Ingredients

2 chopped chicken breasts
1 chopped onion
1 chopped red pepper
2 crushed garlic cloves
4oz chorizo, sliced
1 tbsp Cajun seasoning
2 cup of brown rice
1 tbsp olive oil
12oz of tinned chopped tomatoes
1.5 cup chicken stock

How to make:

1. Grab a large pan and add the olive oil and heat on a medium heat.
2. Add the chicken and brown for around 8 minutes. Place to one side.
3. Add the onion to the pan and fry until tender. Get the garlic, chorizo, Cajun seasoning and red pepper and add to the pan and cook for around 5 minutes.
4. Add the brown rice along with the chopped tomatoes, chicken and chicken stock to the pan. Cover the pan and let simmer for around 25 minutes or until the rice is soft.

(Serves 4)

Calories per serving: 286, Protein: 30g, Carbs: 61g, Fat: 14g

SPICY CHICKEN TRAY-BAKE

A very simple to make chicken recipe that tastes great and contains all the necessary muscle building nutrients.

Ingredients

4 skinless chicken breasts
3 tbsp harissa paste
2 cup of low-fat natural yogurt
1 small, chopped and peeled butternut squash
2 chopped red onions
1 tbsp olive oil

How to make:

1. Pre-heat oven (375°F/190 °C/Gas Mark 5).
2. Add 3 tbsp of yogurt and 2 tbsp of the harissa to a bowl and mix together. Coat the chicken breast with the mixture and leave to one side.
3. Add the onions, chopped butternut squash, 1 tbsp of harissa and 2 tbsp of olive oil to a tray and place in the oven and cook for around 10 minutes. Take the tray out of the oven and add the chicken breast to the tray. Place back in the oven and cook for around 20 minutes until the chicken is cooked right through.
4. Plate up and serve with the leftover yogurt.

(Serves 4)

Calories per serving: 276, Protein: 40g, Carbs: 14g, Fat: 7g

HEALTHY TURKEY BURGERS

Get your burger fix with this healthy turkey alternative.

Ingredients

20oz of mince turkey
1 onion, finely chopped
1 chopped romaine lettuce
4 wholemeal buns
2 diced tomatoes
1 crushed garlic clove
1 lemon
3 tbsp grated parmesan
Chopped parsley
3 tbsp low-fat Greek yogurt

How to make:

1. Pre-heat oven (375°F/190 °C/Gas Mark 5).
2. In a bowl, add the crushed garlic, 2 tbsp of parmesan and parsley.
3. Cut the lemon in half and squeeze the lemon juice over the ingredients. Mix all the ingredients together.
4. Add the ingredients to the minced turkey along with the onion and mix them together.
5. Using your hands, mould the mince mixture into 4 burgers and place on a tray and then cook for around 20 minutes or until the burgers have cooked right through.
6. While the burgers are cooking, cut open the whole-wheat buns and mix the yogurt with the lettuce. Add the burgers to the buns along with the yogurt-lettuce mixture and tomatoes.

(Serves 4)

Calories per serving: 362, Protein: 38g, Carbs: 39g, Fat: 7g

TURKEY MEATBALL FIESTA

Healthy turkey meatballs with added oats to keep you building muscle and burning fat.

Ingredients

20oz of turkey mince
1/2 cup rolled porridge oats
2 chopped spring onions
1 tsp ground cumin
1 tsp coriander
Handful of chopped coriander
1 tsp olive oil
1 chopped red onion
2 chopped garlic cloves
1 large chopped yellow pepper
3 tsp chipotle chilli paste
1 cup chicken stock
16oz of canned chopped tomatoes
16oz of drained black beans
1 avocado, stoned, peeled and chopped

How to make:

1. Add the mince to a bowl with the oats, chopped spring onions, spices and coriander and mix together.
2. Mould the mince mixture into 12 small 'meatballs' using your hands.
3. Add some olive oil to the pan on a medium heat; add the meatballs and cook them until golden.
4. Take them from the pan and leave to one side.
5. Add the onion, chopped pepper and chopped garlic to the pan and cook until tender.
6. Add the chilli paste and ground cumin and chicken stock to the pan and stir well. Then add the meatballs back into the pan.
7. Cover and cook on a low/medium heat for around 10 minutes.
8. Add the tomatoes and black beans to the pan and cook uncovered for around 2-3 minutes.
9. Serve with the chopped avocado and coriander.

(Serves 4)

Calories per serving: 315, Protein: 35g, Carbs: 23g, Fat: 10g

ANABOLIC RATATOUILLE CHICKEN

A tasty low-carb chicken recipe to keep you building muscle and burning fat.

Ingredients

4 chicken breasts
1 chopped onion,
2 chopped red peppers
1 courgette, cut into chunks
1 small aubergine, cut into chunks
4 chopped tomatoes
4 tbsp of olive oil
A pinch of salt and pepper

How to make:

1. Pre-heat oven (375°F/190 °C/Gas Mark 5).
2. Add all the vegetables and the tomatoes to a tray and drizzle with 3 tbsp. olive oil.
3. Place the chicken breasts over the vegetables and season with the remaining tbsp of olive oil and some salt and pepper.
4. Place the tray in the oven and cook for around 30 minutes.
5. Plate up and serve

(Serves 4)

Calories per serving: 324, Protein: 38g, Carbs: 10g, Fat: 15g

BRAWNY CHICKEN CHASSEUR

A classic and tasty chicken dish, packed with protein and low in carbs.

Ingredients

8 chopped rashers of turkey bacon
4 chopped chicken breasts
1 cup of baby mushrooms
1 tbsp plain flour
16oz of canned chopped tomatoes
1 beef stock cube
1 tbsp Worcestershire sauce
Handful of chopped parsley
1 tbsp olive oil

How to make:

1. Heat the olive oil on a medium heat in a shallow saucepan and add the turkey bacon and cook for 4-5 minutes until it starts to brown.
2. Add the chopped chicken breasts and cook for around 5 minutes until golden. Increase the heat to high and add the baby mushrooms for 2 minutes. Add the flour and stir in until a paste starts to form.
3. Add the canned chopped tomatoes and beef stock cube to the saucepan and cook for around 10 minutes.
4. Then add the parsley and Worcestershire sauce to the pan, stir in and then serve.

(Serves 4)

Calories per serving: 242, Protein: 50g, Carbs: 5g, Fat: 3g

AESTHETIC TOMATO AND OLIVE PAN-FRIED CHICKEN

A tasty chicken dish, sure to satisfy your hunger and nutritional needs.

Ingredients

2 chicken breasts
1 chopped onion,
2 chopped garlic cloves
16oz of canned chopped tomatoes
1 tbsp balsamic vinegar
6 chopped green olives
1 cup of chicken stock
2 tbsp olive oil
Handful of basil leaves
A pinch of salt and pepper

How to make:

1. Heat olive oil on a medium heat in a pan.
2. Sprinkle some salt and pepper over the chicken and then place the chicken in the pan and cook for roughly 10 minutes, or until the chicken has cooked right through..
3. Add the onion to the pan and turn the chicken over and cook for another 4 – 5 minutes. Remove the chicken from the pan and place to one side.
4. Add the garlic to the pan and continue to cook the onions until tender.
5. Add the chopped tomatoes, olives, chicken stock and balsamic vinegar to the pan with most of the basil leaves and turn down the heat, simmering for around 8 minutes.
6. Place the chicken back into the pan, cover and simmer for a further 5 minutes
7. Plate up and serve with the remaining basil as a garnish.

(Serves 2)

Calories per serving: 334, Protein: 39g, Carbs: 8g, Fat: 19g

CHICKEN BRAWN BURGER

Another great healthy burger alternative! Quick and easy to make if you're strapped for time. Contains a good helping of protein to keep you anabolic.

Ingredients

1 chicken breast
1 tbsp low fat mayonnaise
1 chopped red onion
1 chopped lettuce
1 slice of low-fat cheddar
1 whole wheat burger bun
1 tsp of chopped jalapeno slices
1 tsp olive oil

How to make:

1. Heat olive oil on a medium heat in a griddle pan.
2. Cover the chicken breast with some salt and pepper and add to the pan and cook for around 5 minutes. Turn it over and cook for a further 5 minutes.
3. Add the slice of cheddar to the top of the chicken. Cook chicken for another 8 minutes or until chicken is cooked right through.
4. Remove chicken from pan and place to one side.
5. Cut open the roll and add the chicken, onions, mayonnaise, lettuce and chopped jalapeno.

(Serves 1)

Calories per serving: 458, Protein: 50g, Carbs: 38g, Fat: 12g

TASTY TURKEY BAGEL

A great recipe, ideal for lunch or post-work-out! Contains lots of protein to keep you growing.

Ingredients

2 thick deli turkey breast slices (cooked)
1 whole-wheat bagel
Handful of baby spinach
Handful of rocket
1 chopped tomato
¼ sliced cucumber

How to make:

1. Cut the whole-wheat bagel in half and then add each half to the toaster.
2. Add the turkey breast, chopped tomato, cucumber, spinach and rocket to the bagel.
3. Serve on the go or at home!

(Serves 1)

Calories per serving: 336, Protein: 21g, Carbs: 64g, Fat: 1g

DICED CHICKEN WITH EGG NOODLES

Go ahead and mix things up with this tasty recipe. Contains the right amount of protein, carbs and fats to meet your goals.

Ingredients

6oz of chopped chicken breast
1/2 cup of whole-wheat noodles
1 grated carrot
2 tbsp of fresh orange juice
1 tsp of sesame seeds
3 tsp of soy sauce
2 tsp of rapeseed oil
1 chopped ginger
1 cup of sugar snap peas

How to make:

1. Heat 1 tsp rapeseed oil on a medium heat in pan.
2. Cook the chopped chicken breast for about 10-15 minutes or until cooked through.
3. While cooking the chicken, place the noodles in a pot of boiling water for about 5 minutes.
4. In a bowl, mix together the ginger, sesame seeds, soy sauce, 1 tsp rapeseed oil and orange juice.
5. Once chicken is cooked and noodles are cooked and drained, add the chicken, noodles, carrot and peas to the dressing and mix.

(Serves 2)

Calories per serving: 332, Protein: 30g, Carbs: 31g, Fat: 8g

HONEY GLAZED GROWTH CHICKEN

Mix things up with this sweet and tempting chicken recipe.

Ingredients

2 chicken breasts with skin on
½ lemon
1 tbsp honey
1 tbsp dark soy sauce
A pinch of salt and pepper

How to make:

1. Pre-heat oven (375°F/190 °C/Gas Mark 5).
2. Place the chicken breast on a baking dish and add a sprinkle of salt and pepper.
3. Get a bowl and squeeze the lemon juice in and add the honey and soy sauce. Mix the ingredients together and cover the chicken breasts with it.
4. Place the squeezed lemon in between the chicken breasts and place the dish into the oven and cook for around 30 minutes on until fully cooked through.

(Serves 2)

Calories per serving: 195, Protein: 37g, Carbs: 9g, Fat: 2g

MIGHTY MEXICAN CHICKEN STEW

Spice things up with this classic Mexican chicken stew. Packed full of protein from the chicken as well as the quinoa!

Ingredients

4 skinless chicken breasts
1 cup quinoa
16oz of drained pinto beans
1 tbsp olive oil
1 chopped onion
2 chopped red peppers
3 tbsp chipotle paste
32oz of tinned chopped tomatoes
2 chicken stock cubes
Handful of chopped coriander
1 lime

How to make:

1. Heat olive oil on a medium heat in a deep pan and add the onion and peppers and cook for 2-3 minutes.
2. Then add the chipotle paste and the tinned chopped tomatoes.
3. Add the chicken breast and add just enough water to cover the chicken by 1cm and then bring down the heat to let the mixture simmer. Cook for around 20 minutes until the chicken is cooked right through.
4. Add boiling water to a separate saucepan along with stock cubes. Pour in the quinoa and heat for around 12 minutes.
5. Add the pinto beans and cook for a further 3 minutes. Drain the quinoa and add in the coriander and squeeze the lime juice in - mix and place to one side.
6. Serve the chicken with the quinoa and cover with the tomato sauce from the pan.

(Serves 4)

Calories per serving: 464, Protein: 51g, Carbs: 53g, Fat: 4g

SPICY CAJUN CHICKEN WITH GUACAMOLE

Tasty low fat, low carb chicken recipe! Contains a generous amount of protein to keep you building muscle and burning fat.

Ingredients

4 chicken breasts
1 tbsp paprika
1 tsp dried onion flakes
¼ tsp cayenne pepper
2 tsp dried thyme
A pinch of salt and pepper
1 tbsp olive oil
1 cup of guacamole

How to make:

1. Get a bowl and add the cayenne pepper, dried thyme, paprika, salt, pepper and onion flakes and mix together.
2. Get the chicken and cut two deep scores on each breast. Rub the oil onto the chicken then cover the breasts with the spices.
3. Add the chicken to the grill and cook for around 8 minutes each side or until completely cooked through.
4. Serve chicken with the guacamole

(Serves 4)

Calories per serving: 190, Protein: 34g, Carbs: 3g, Fat: 5g

MUSCLE CHICKEN CACCIATORE

An Italian inspired, delicious, low fat, low carb chicken recipe. Contains a liberal amount of protein to keep you building muscle and burning fat.

Ingredients

4 chicken breasts
1 chopped onion
2 sliced garlic cloves
A pinch of salt and pepper
1 tsp olive oil
14oz of tinned chopped tomatoes
2 tbsp chopped rosemary leaves
Handful of basil leaves

How to make:

1. Pre-Heat oven (375°F/190 °C/Gas Mark 5).
2. Heat oil in a pan on a medium heat and add the onion and garlic and cook until soft.
3. Pour in the chopped tomatoes, rosemary, salt and pepper and cook for around 15 minutes until the mixture has become thicker.
4. Spread the mixture over the chicken; place the chicken on a tray and transfer to the oven. Leave in the oven for 20 minutes until the chicken is cooked right through. Sprinkle the basil over the chicken and serve.

(Serves 4)

Calories per serving: 172, Protein: 33g, Carbs: 6g, Fat: 2g

ARTICHOKE & TOMATO CHICKEN BAKE

A taste of the Mediterranean!

Ingredients

4X skinless chicken thighs
1 Onion, roughly chopped
2 Garlic cloves, chopped
2 Cans chopped tomatoes
1 Tbsp balsamic vinegar
1/2 Cup jarred artichokes
1 Cup homemade chicken stock
1 Bay leaf
A pinch of black pepper
1 Cup brown rice

How to make:

1. Preheat oven to 375°F/190 °C/Gas Mark 5.
2. Add the onion, garlic, chopped tomatoes, artichoke, chicken stock, balsamic vinegar and the bay leaf to a baking dish and cover.
3. Place in the oven for 35-40 minutes or until chicken is thoroughly cooked.
4. Meanwhile add the rice to a pan of water and bring to the boil.
5. Lower the heat and simmer for 20 minutes or until most of the water is absorbed.
6. Drain, return the lid and steam for 5 minutes.
7. Plate up and serve with a pinch of black pepper and brown rice.

(Serves 2)

Calories per serving: 695, Protein: 49g, Carbs: 55g, Fat: 33g

CAJUN CHICKEN

Scrumptious!

Ingredients

2X skinless chicken breasts, sliced
1 Red onion, chopped
1 Green pepper, chopped
2 Garlic cloves, crushed
1 Tsp cayenne pepper
1 Tsp chili powder
1/4 Tsp chili powder
1 Tsp dried oregano
1 Tsp dried thyme
1 Cup brown rice
1 Tbsp extra virgin olive oil
1/2 Can chopped tomatoes
1 Cup homemade chicken stock

How to make:

1. Pre-Heat oven (375°F/190 °C/Gas Mark 5).
2. Heat oil in a pan on a medium heat and add the onion and garlic and cook until soft.
3. Pour in the chopped tomatoes, rosemary, salt and pepper and cook for around 15 minutes until the mixture has become thicker.
4. Spread the mixture over the chicken; place the chicken on a tray and transfer to the oven. Leave in the oven for 20 minutes until the chicken is cooked right through. Sprinkle the basil over the chicken and serve.

(Serves 4)

Calories per serving: 172, Protein: 33g, Carbs: 6g, Fat: 2g

CHICKEN BURGERS & GUACAMOLE

Healthy chicken burgers with wholemeal pittas.

Ingredients

2X skinless chicken breasts
1 Tsp oregano
1 Tsp paprika
1 Tsp garlic salt
2 X wholemeal pitta breads
1 Avocado
1/4 Cup greek yogurt
1/2 Lime, juiced
1/4 Cup spinach leaves, washed
1 Tomato, sliced

How to make:

1. Preheat the broiler to a medium high heat.
2. Slice the chicken breasts in half lengthways.
3. Mix the herbs and spices together and sprinkle over the chicken breasts.
4. Add the chicken to a baking tray and broil for 20-25 minutes or until thoroughly cooked through.
5. Meanwhile, peel and slice the avocado and add to the natural yogurt with the lime juice. Use your fork to mush these together to form the guacamole. Season with a little black pepper.
6. Lightly toast the pitta breads and then stuff each with a chicken breast, spinach leaves, tomato and a dollop of guacamole.
7. Enjoy!

(Serves 2)

Calories per serving: 410, Protein: 35g, Carbs: 55g, Fat: 17g

DIVINE DUCK BREASTS

Chinese spiced duck breasts.

Ingredients

1 Tsp coconut oil
2 Duck breasts, skin removed
2 Green onions, sliced
3 Garlic cloves, minced
2 Tsp ginger, grated
1 Tsp nutmeg
1 Tsp cloves
1 Orange – zest and juice (reserve the wedges)
2 Bok or pak choi plants, leaves separated

How to make:

1. Slice the duck breasts into strips and add to a dry hot pan, cooking for 5-7 minutes on each side or until cooked through to your liking.
2. Remove to one side.
3. Add oil to a clean pan and sauté the onions with the ginger, garlic and the rest of the spices for 1 minute.
4. Add the juice and zest of the orange and continue to sauté for 3-5 minutes.
5. Add the duck and bok choi and heat through until wilted and duck is piping hot.
6. Serve and garnish with the orange segments.

(Serves 2)

Calories per serving: 230, Protein: 28g, Carbs: 15g, Fat: 17g

TASTY TURKEY BURGERS

Lean and mouthwatering!

Ingredients

10 Oz lean ground turkey meat
1 White onion, minced
1 Carrot, shredded
2 Celery stalks, finely chopped
1 Tbsp parsley
1 Tsp cilantro
1 Tsp dry mustard
2 Tbsp olive oil
Pinch of black pepper to taste
2 Wholegrain buns
1/2 Cup arugula

How to make:

1. Pre-heat oven to 390°F/200 °C/Gas Mark 6.
2. Add the vegetables in a bowl with the olive oil, pepper and herbs and then mix well.
3. Add in the meat and mix with wet hands to create two burgers.
4. Place the burgers on a lightly oiled baking tray and bake in the oven for 25-30 minutes or until meat is cooked through (flip half way).
5. Turn up the broiler and broil for the last 5 minutes for a golden and crispy edge.
6. Serve in the buns with arugula.

(Serves 2)

Calories per serving: 230, Protein: 28g, Carbs: 15g, Fat: 17g

OVEN-BAKED CHICKEN THIGHS

An exciting take on your usual bland chicken meals.

Ingredients

4 Chicken thighs
2 Sweet potatoes, peeled and chopped
2 Red onions, chopped
1/2 Cup greek yogurt
1 Tsp paprika
For the marinade:
1 Red pepper, diced
1 Tsp dried red chilli,
1 Garlic clove, minced
1 Tsp basil, chopped
1 Tbsp tomato purée (no added salt or sugar)
1 Tbsp extra virgin olive oil

How to make:

1. Pre-heat oven to 375°F/190 °C/Gas Mark 5.
2. In a bowl, combine the ingredients for the marinade.
3. Coat the chicken with the mixture, cover and leave to one side.
4. Pour the chicken pieces, onions and sweet potato, with the leftover marinade juices over a baking tray and place in the oven for 35 minutes or until the chicken is thoroughly cooked through.
5. Add the yogurt to a serving bowl and sprinkle paprika over the top.
6. Plate up the chicken and vegetables with the yogurt dressing.

(Serves 4)

Calories per serving: 230, Protein: 28g, Carbs: 15g, Fat: 17g

NOURISHING NUTTY NOODLES

These are great for lunch or dinner and taste like a cheat meal!

Ingredients

2 Skinless chicken breasts, sliced
1 Cup noodles
1 Carrot, chopped
1 Lime, juiced
1 Tbsp cashew nuts, crushed
2 Tsp coconut oil
1/2 Cup broccoli florets
1/2 Cup mushrooms

How to make:

1. Heat 1 tsp oil on a medium heat in a skillet.
2. Sauté the chicken breasts for about 10-15 minutes or until cooked through.
3. While cooking the chicken, place the noodles, carrots and broccoli in a pot of boiling water for 5 minutes. Drain.
4. In a bowl, mix together 1 tsp oil, lime juice and crushed cashew nuts to make your dressing.
5. Add all of the ingredients to the dressing and toss through.
6. Serve warm straight away or chill in airtight container for a go-to lunch.

(Serves 2)

Calories per serving: 403, Protein: 31g, Carbs: 27g, Fat: 18g
=

TRAINING TURKEY KEBABS

Turkey is lean and full of protein and tastes delicious in this kebab recipe with salsa.

Ingredients

1 Lemon, juiced
2 Garlic cloves, minced
1 Tsp cumin
1 Tsp turmeric
4 Turkey breasts, cut into cubes
4 Metal kebab skewers
Lemon wedges to garnisH
1 Red onion, diced
1 Beef tomato, diced
1 Lemon, juiced
1 Tsp white wine vinegar
1 Tsp black pepper
1 Tbsp olive oil

How to make:

1. Whisk the lemon juice, garlic, cumin and turmeric in a bowl.
2. Skewer the turkey cubes using kebab sticks (metal).
3. Baste the turkey on each side with the marinade, covering for as long as possible in the fridge (don't worry if you don't have time to wait - these can be cooked straight away).
4. When ready to cook, preheat the oven to 400°F/200 °C/Gas Mark 6 and bake for 20-25 minutes or until turkey is thoroughly cooked through.
5. Prepare the salsa by mixing all the ingredients in a separate bowl.
6. Serve the turkey kebabs, garnished with the lemon wedges and the salsa on the side.

(Serves 4)

Calories per serving: 193, Protein: 34g, Carbs: 9g, Fat: 9g

CARROT NOODLES & CILANTRO CHICKEN

Go easy on the carbs with this flavorsome pasta dish.

Ingredients

For the chicken:

2 Skinless chicken breasts, sliced
1 Tbsp extra virgin olive oil
Juice of 1/2 lemon
1 Clove garlic, crushed
1 Tbsp cilantro, chopped
Pinch of black pepper

For the pasta:

5 Carrots, peeled
1 Tsp extra virgin olive oil
1 Tbsp sesame seeds (optional)

How to make:

1. Pre-heat oven to 400°F/200°C/Gas Mark 6.
2. Combine 1 tbsp olive oil, lemon juice and garlic and coat the chicken slices.
3. Line a baking sheet with foil or parchment paper.
4. Layer the chicken strips and cook for 25-30 minutes or until cooked through.
5. Meanwhile, prepare your carrots by using a spiralyzer to create noodles. Alternatively use a sharp knife to cut long vertical strips from the carrot.
6. When chicken is cooked, remove from the oven and place to one side.
7. Boil a pan of water on a medium heat and add a pinch of black pepper.
8. Add your carrot to the water and boil for one minute before immediately draining.
9. Plate and serve, layering half the chicken on top and drizzling with 1 tsp olive oil , sesame seeds and cilantro.
10. Enjoy!

(Serves 2)

Calories per serving: 310, Protein: 25g, Carbs: 5g, Fat: 20g

POWERFUL PESTO CHICKEN

Italian inspired chicken dish.

Ingredients

2 Chicken breasts
1 Cup fresh basil
1 Cup watercress
1/2 Cup walnuts
2 Tbsp extra virgin olive oil
1/2 Cup low fat hard cheese (Optional)
1 Cup brown rice

How to make:

1. Preheat oven to 350°f/170°c/Gas Mark 4.
2. Add the rice to a pan of cold water over a high heat and cook for 20 minutes.
3. Meanwhile, take the chicken breasts and use a meat pounder to 'thin' each breast into a 1cm thick escalope.
4. Reserve a handful of the nuts before adding the rest of the ingredients and a little black pepper to a blender or pestle and mortar and blend until smooth.
5. Add a little water if the pesto needs loosening.
6. Coat the chicken in the pesto.
7. Bake for at least 30 minutes in the oven, or until chicken is completely cooked through.
8. Once rice has soaked up most of the water, drain and place the lid on the pan. Allow to steam.
9. Serve the chicken escalopes with the brown rice and sprinkle with the extra nuts to serve.

(Serves 2)

Calories per serving: 310, Protein: 40g, Carbs: 25g, Fat: 35g

MEDITERRANEAN CHICKEN & EGGPLANT

Yummy! .

Ingredients

4X 4oz skinless chicken breasts or thighs
1 Red onion, chopped
2 Garlic cloves, chopped
2 Eggplants, peeled & chopped into chunks
1 Tbsp balsamic vinegar
1 Tbsp extra virgin olive oil
2 Tbsp oregano, fresh or dried
2 Tbsp basil
2 Whole lemons
1/4 Cup water
A pinch of black pepper

How to make:

1. Preheat the oven to 375°F/190°C/Gas Mark 5.
2. Add chicken, onion, garlic and eggplant to a lined baking tray and sprinkle over herbs and black pepper.
3. Pour over the water, olive oil and balsamic vinegar, so that the chicken and vegetables are sitting in a shallow bath.
4. Cut 1 lemon in half and add to the baking tray.
5. Bake in the oven for 35-40 minutes or until chicken is completely cooked through.
6. Serve the chicken and eggplant with a wedge of lemon each.

7. Sprinkle with freshly torn basil and black pepper to serve.
8. Enjoy with your choice of brown rice or pasta.

(Serves 4)

Calories per serving: 175, Protein: 25g, Carbs: 3g, Fat: 5g

BODYBUILDING FAJITAS

A healthy version of the takeaway favorite.

Ingredients

1 Iceberg lettuce
1 Tsp olive oil
24 Oz ground lean turkey
1/2 Onion, finely diced
1 Red pepper, finely diced
1 Tsp paprika

How to make:

1. Carefully pull off the cabbage leaves from the lettuce, wash and leave intact.
2. Mix the rest of the ingredients in a bowl and divide into quarters.
3. Heat the oil in a skillet over a medium to high heat.
4. Add the turkey mixture to the pan and cook for 15-20 minutes or until cooked through.
5. Once cooked, remove from the pan and add to the centre of each lettuce leaf before wrapping fajitas style!
6. Enjoy.

(Serves 4)

Calories per serving: 205, Protein: 21g, Carbs: 17g, Fat: 17g

MIGHTY STUFFED PEPPERS

This is a filling and healthy treat!

Ingredients

2 Large red bell peppers, cut in half
5oz lean ground chicken
1 Cup cooked quinoa
1 Tbsp cayenne pepper
1 Tbsp parsley
1 Tsp black pepper
1/2 Red onion, finely diced
1 Clove garlic, minced

How to make:

1. Preheat the oven to 350°f/170°c/Gas Mark 4.
2. Remove seeds from the middle of the bell peppers and layer onto a baking tray.
3. Combine the turkey mince with the onion, garlic, herbs, spices and quinoa.
4. Stuff the peppers with the mixture.
5. Add to the oven for 30-40 minutes or until turkey is cooked through.

(Serves 2)

Calories per serving: 470, Protein: 25g, Carbs: 65g, Fat: 11g

CARIBBEAN TURKEY THIGHS

Try this homemade jerk recipe to keep you pumping!

Ingredients

4x turkey thighs
1/4 Cup honey
1 Tbsp mustard
2 Tsp curry powder
1 Garlic clove, minced
1 Tbsp jamaican spice blend
1 Lime
1 Cup brown rice
1/2 Cup canned kidney beans

How to make:

1. Preheat the oven to 350°f/170°c/Gas Mark 4.
2. Prepare marinade by mixing butter, honey, mustard, garlic and spices and pour over the chicken.
3. Add the turkey and the marinade to a baking dish and place in oven for 35-40 minutes.
4. Meanwhile prepare your rice by bringing a pan of water to the boil, add rice and beans.
5. Cover and simmer for 20 minutes.
6. Drain and cover the rice and return to the stove for 5 minutes.
7. When turkey is cooked through, serve on a bed of rice and beans and squeeze fresh lime juice over the top.
8. Enjoy.

(Serves 4)

Calories per serving: 575, Protein: 65g, Carbs: 24g, Fat: 22g

CHICKEN WITH HOMEMADE SLAW

Hit your PB with this great dish.

Ingredients

2 Chicken Breasts
1/2 Lemon, Juiced
1 Tsp Black Pepper
1 Tsp Oregano
For The Slaw:
1/2 Red Cabbage
1 Carrot
1/2 Lemon, Juiced
5 Radishes, Sliced
1 Tbsp Cilantro, Chopped

How to make:

1. Preheat the broiler on a medium to high heat.
2. Cut each chicken breast in half and add to a sheet of baking paper with the pepper, lemon juice and herbs.
3. Place under the broiler for 20-25 minutes or until chicken is thoroughly cooked through. Turn once during cooking.
4. Meanwhile, prepare your slaw: Peel the carrot and grate or spiralyze.
5. Cut cabbage into very thin slices.
6. Mix all of the ingredients for the slaw in a separate bowl and toss.
7. Serve the chicken with the slaw and your choice of carbs if needed.

(Serves 2)

Calories per serving: 168, Protein: 27g, Carbs: 4g, Fat: 4g

CHEEKY CHICKEN CURRY

Spicy and aromatic curry.

Ingredients

1 Tbsp coconut oil
1 Tsp garam masala
1 Tsp cumin
1 Tsp turmeric
1/2 Chili, finely diced
1/2 Onion, diced
1 Clove garlic, minced
1 Zucchini, peeled & sliced
1/2 Cup chopped tomatoes, no added salt or sugar
1 Cup water
2 Chicken thighs/drumsticks
2 Tbsp fresh cilantro, finely chopped
1 Cup brown rice
1/4 Cup greek yogurt

How to make:

1. Heat oil in a pan on a medium heat and add onions, stirring for 3-4 minutes until they begin to soften.
2. Add spices one by one and stir for 4-5 minutes, releasing the flavors.
3. Now add the garlic and chili and stir.
4. Add the tomatoes and water to the pan and stir thoroughly.
5. Now add the chicken, cover and simmer for 35-40 minutes until chicken is completely cooked through.
6. Add the zucchini in the last 15 minutes.
7. Meanwhile prepare your rice by bringing a pan of water to the boil, adding rice and covering and simmering for 20 minutes.
8. Drain and cover the rice and return to the stove for 5 minutes.
9. Plate up individual rice portions and the chicken curry over the top.
10. Add a dollop of yogurt and fresh cilantro to serve.

(Serves 2)

Calories per serving: 338, Protein: 32g, Carbs: 34g, Fat: 7g

LEMON CHICKEN WITH SWEDE & KALE PUREE

Lean and fresh.

Ingredients

2 Chicken breasts, skinless
1 Lemon, juiced
1 Tsp oregano
1 Tsp black pepper
1 Tsp olive oil
1 Swede
1 Tsp paprika
1 Tsp chili powder
2 Metal kebab sticks
1 Cup kale
1/2 Green pepper

How to make:

1. Mix the oil, lemon juice, oregano and black pepper to form a marinade.
2. Cut the chicken breasts into bite-size cubes and marinate for as long as time permits.
3. Preheat the broiler on a medium to high heat.
4. Cut the green pepper into bites-size pieces.
5. Skewer the chicken and pepper alternately.
6. Add the kebabs to a lined baking tray and broil for 20-25 minutes or until thoroughly cooked through.
7. Meanwhile, wash, peel and dice the swede into small pieces.
8. Place a pan of water on a high heat and bring to

the boil.

9. Add the swede, paprika and chili powder.
10. Lower the heat and allow to cook for 20 minutes or until soft.
11. Add the kale to steam over the top for 10-15 minutes.
12. Once swede is soft and chicken is cooked, remove the chicken and place to one side.
13. Drain the swede and kale and place in a blender for 30 seconds or until puréed.
14. Add a little salt and pepper to taste here and serve with the lemon chicken kebabs.

(Serves 2)

Calories per serving: 312, Protein: 27g, Carbs: 10g, Fat: 15g

TOMATO, MOZZARELLA & BASIL CHICKEN

Melt in the middle chicken thighs.

Ingredients

4 X Boneless & Skinless Chicken Thighs
1 Cup Mozzarella
2 Beef Tomatoes, Halved
4 Tsp Fresh Basil
1 Tbsp Black Pepper
4 Cocktail Sticks
1/2 Cup Olives, Pitted & Sliced
1 Tsp Olive Oil

How to make:

1. Preheat the oven to 350°f/170°c/Gas Mark 4.
2. Unfold the chicken thigh to fan it out flat.
3. Stuff with 1/4 mozzarella, tomato, olives and basil.
4. Fold the thigh back over and pierce through the middle with a cocktail stick.
5. Season with black pepper and drizzle with olive oil.
6. Wrap in foil or baking paper.
7. Add to a baking dish in the oven and bake for 30-35 minutes or until cooked through.
8. Serve 2 thighs each with your choice of side.

(Serves 4)

Calories per serving: 300, Protein: 34g, Carbs: 4g, Fat: 15g

TURKEY & CRANBERRY SAUCE

A Christmas fave that can be enjoyed all year round!

Ingredients

2 X turkey breasts
1 Cup cranberries
1 Tsp nutmeg
1 Tsp cinammon
1 Tsp black pepper
1 Cup water
1 Tsp red wine vinegar

How to make:

1. Preheat the broiler to a medium heat.
2. Butterfly the turkey breast with a sharp knife and season with a little black pepper.
3. Add to a lined baking dish and broil for 25-30 minutes or until cooked through.
4. Meanwhile, heat a pot on a medium to high heat and add the rest of the ingredients.
5. Allow to boil and then turn down the heat and simmer for 15 minutes or until reduced to a thick sauce.
6. Serve the turkey breasts once cooked with a helping of cranberry sauce and your choice of veg.

(Serves 2)

Calories per serving: 200, Protein: 34g, Carbs: 10g, Fat: 2g

TANDOORI STYLE CHICKEN DRUMSTICKS

Tastes amazing with the mint dip.

Ingredients

4 X chicken drumsticks, skinless
1 Tsp turmeric
1 Tsp cumin
1 Tsp garam masala
1/2 White onion, thinly sliced
1 Garlic clove, minced
1 Cup cooked brown rice
1 Tsp coconut oil
1 Tsp canola oil
2 Tbsp fresh mint, chopped
1/2 Cup greek yogurt
1/4 Cucumber, finely diced
1 Tsp curry powder

How to make:

1. Mix the spices and garlic together with the canola oil and marinate the chicken for as long as you can.
2. Heat a large pan on a medium heat.
3. Add coconut oil until melted.
4. Add the onions for 4-5 minutes or until soft.
5. Now add the chicken drumsticks and cook for 25-30 minutes or until cooked through.
6. Meanwhile, mix the yogurt, mint, cucumber and curry powder in a small bowl and place to one side.
7. Serve with brown rice and a helping of the mint dip.

(Serves 2)

Calories per serving: 625, Protein: 51g, Carbs: 37g, Fat: 29g

TURKEY MEATBALLS & COUSCOUS

Juicy meatballs served with a herby side.

Ingredients

10 Oz ground turkey
1 Egg white
1/4 Cup canned tomatoes
1/2 Lemon, juiced
1 Tsp black pepper
2 Tbsp fresh parsley, chopped
1 Cup couscous
1 Tbsp olive oil
1 Tbsp crushed almonds
1 Tsp balsamic vinegar
1/2 Onion, diced
1 Garlic clove, minced

How to make:

1. Mix the ground turkey with the egg white, black pepper, balsamic vinegar and 1 tbsp parsley.
2. Use your hands to shape into meatballs.
3. Heat the oil in a skillet over a medium to high heat.
4. Add the onions and garlic and saute until soft (4-5 minutes).
5. Now add the meatballs and brown each side.
6. Add the chopped tomatoes and allow to cook for 15-20 minutes or until meat is thoroughly cooked through.
7. Meanwhile, add the couscous to a bowl and pour over boiling water to just cover the couscous.
8. Cover and allow to steam for 5 minutes.
9. Now add 1 tbsp parsley, lemon juice and crushed nuts.
10. Serve the meatballs (the sauce should be reduced to a thick sauce by now) over the couscous.

(Serves 2)

Calories per serving: 460, Protein: 35g, Carbs: 35g, Fat: 21g

CHICKEN WITH HOMEMADE CHIPOTLE SAUCE

Smoky and spicy greatness, helping you build muscle.

Ingredients

4 free range chicken thighs (grilled)
7-10 chipotle peppers (stems removed and cut lengthways)
1 cup organic tomatoes (skin removed and blended)
1.5 cup of water or homemade chicken broth
2 tbsp apple cider vinegar
1 white onion (minced)
2 cloves garlic (minced)
2 tbsp organic honey
1/2 tsp sea salt
1/2 tsp cumin
1 tsp cinnamon
1 tsp paprika

How to make:

1. Simmer all ingredients except the peppers and chicken thighs in a pan for 30 minutes (you could double up the ingredients and freeze half for future dipping!)
2. Add the peppers and simmer for another 30 minutes without the lid on.
3. Pour the sauce over the grilled chicken thighs.
4. Plate up and serve.

(Serves 2)

Calories per serving: 585, Protein: 55g, Carbs: 17g, Fat: 33g

GRILLED CHICKEN KEBABS

A power-protein snack for the paleo palette; contains a whopping 73 grams of protein!

Ingredients

2 chicken breasts (free range)
2 minced garlic cloves
1 chopped red chilli (deseeded)
2 tbsp of sesame oil
1 red onion, chopped into eight pieces
Sprinkle of salt and pepper
3 wooden skewers

How to make:

1. Chop the chicken breasts into chunky pieces using a sharp knife or scissors.
2. Mix the sesame oil with the minced garlic, chilli and salt and pepper (as desired).
3. Marinate the chicken in half the oil and leave for at least one hour - if possible leave to marinate overnight.
4. Keep the rest of the oil for brushing whilst cooking.
5. Heat the grill to a high heat and soak wooden skewers in water.
6. Take skewers from the water and pierce a chunk of chicken followed by a slice of red onion – repeat this until skewer is covered.
7. Grill for 15-20 minutes, using a brush to rub the remaining oil over the chicken every five minutes and turning throughout.
8. Check there is no pink inside the chicken when cut and that it is boiling hot before serving).

(Serves 1)

Calories per serving: 488, Protein: 73g, Carbs: 10g, Fat: 17g

SUPER STICKY CHICKEN CLUBS

Caveman friendly!!

Ingredients

8 chicken drumsticks (free range)
1 tbsp organic honey
1 tbsp olive oil
2 beef tomatoes cut into quarters (organic when possible)
1 tbsp Dijon mustard

How to make:

1. Using a sharp knife, score each of the drumsticks.
2. Mix together the honey, oil, and mustard.
3. Pour this mixture over the chicken and coat thoroughly.
4. Leave to marinate for 30 minutes at room temperature or overnight in the fridge.
5. Preheat oven to (200°C /400°f/Gas Mark 6).
6. Tip the chicken into a shallow roasting tray, add the quartered tomatoes and cook for 35 minutes, turning occasionally, until the chicken is tender and glistening with the marinade.
7. Plate up and serve.

(Serves 4)

Calories per serving: 404, Protein: 47g, Carbs: 37g, Fat: 8g

ANABOLIC RATATOUILLE CHICKEN

A delicious French inspired chicken dish..

Ingredients

4 chicken breasts (free range)
1 chopped onion,
2 chopped red peppers
1 courgette, cut into chunks
1 small aubergine, cut into chunks
4 chopped tomatoes
4 tbsp of olive oil
Sprinkle of salt and pepper

How to make:

1. Pre-heat oven to (200°C /400°f/Gas Mark 6).
2. Add all the vegetables and the tomatoes to a tray and drizzle with 3 tbsp of olive oil.
3. Place the chicken breasts over the vegetables and season with the remaining tbsp of olive oil and some salt and pepper.
4. Place the tray in the oven and cook for 30 minutes or until chicken cooked through.
5. Plate up and serve.

(Serves 4)

Calories per serving: 324, Protein: 38g, Carbs: 10g, Fat: 15g

PALEO CHICKEN MUSHROOM BRAWN BURGER

One healthy burger! It's quick and easy to make if you're low on time, containing a good helping of protein to keep you anabolic.

Ingredients

4 portabella mushrooms (without the stalks)
2 tbsp of coconut oil
2 eggs (free range)
2 chicken breasts (free range)
1 chopped beef tomato
Sprinkle of salt and pepper
½ chopped iceberg lettuce

How to make:

1. Preheat grill on high.
2. Season chicken breasts with salt and pepper.
3. Place chicken in grill and cook for 20 minutes, turning chicken over half way through. Make sure chicken is cooked right through.
4. Heat coconut oil in pan on a medium heat.
5. Add mushrooms and sauté for 5 minutes until mushrooms are tender.
6. Remove mushrooms and place to one side.
7. Add the egg to the pan and fry on a medium heat for 4-5 minutes.
8. Serve the chicken and eggs on top of the two mushroom caps topped again with the lettuce and chopped tomatoes.
9. Plate up and enjoy!

(Serves 1)

Calories per serving: 458, Protein: 50g, Carbs: 38g, Fat: 12g

TANGY ORANGE AND CHICKEN THIGHS

Mix things up with this tangy chicken recipe..

Ingredients

12oz of chicken thighs (free range)
Sprinkle of pepper
Juice of 2 oranges
Juice of 1 lime
2 tbsp of crushed ginger
2 tbsp of olive oil
2 peeled and pieced oranges
2 chopped cloves of garlic
1 chopped green pepper

How to make:

1. Heat oil in a large pan over a medium heat.
2. Season chicken thighs with pepper and add to the frying pan to brown.
3. After the chicken starts to brown, add garlic to the pan and stir for 1 minute.
4. Add the orange juice, ginger, lime, and oranges to the pan and stir well.
5. Cover the pan and bring to a simmer.
6. Cook chicken for around 25-30 minutes or until chicken is cooked through.
7. Plate up and serve.

(Serves 2)

Calories per serving: 555, Protein: 32g, Carbs: 25g, Fat: 35g

SWEET HONEY CHICKEN

Add a little sweet and savoury kick to your favourite protein source...

Ingredients

6 chicken drumsticks (free range)
Sprinkle of salt and pepper
2 tbsp of sesame oil
1 diced red pepper
1 finely diced chilli
1 tbsp of organic honey
3 minced garlic cloves

How to make:

1. In a bowl, add the honey chilli, garlic, diced red pepper, sesame oil, salt and pepper.
2. Mix them together.
3. Pour half of the honey mixture over the chicken drumsticks.
4. Make sure that the drumsticks are covered evenly.
5. Leave the chicken mix to marinate for at least 3 hours or overnight if possible.
6. Preheat the grill to a medium heat when ready.
7. Line a baking tray with tin foil and spread the chicken out evenly.
8. Grill under a medium heat for 25-30 minutes.
9. Check chicken is cooked through and piping hot before serving.
10. Plate up and serve.

(Serves 2)

Calories per serving: 479, Protein: 42g, Carbs: 17g, Fat: 27g

DOUBLE WHAMMY

Contains a double dose of protein to keep you building muscle and burning fat...

Ingredients

30oz of chicken thighs (free range)
4oz of turkey bacon (or pork if you can't find turkey)
1 cup of chicken stock

How to make:

1. Heat oil in a large pan over a medium heat.
2. Season chicken thighs with pepper and add to the frying pan to brown.
3. After the chicken starts to brown, add garlic to the pan and stir for 1 minute.
4. Add the orange juice, ginger, lime, and oranges to the pan and stir well.
5. Cover the pan and bring to a simmer.
6. Cook chicken for around 25-30 minutes or until chicken is cooked through.
7. Plate up and serve.

(Serves 4)

**Calories per serving: 190 , Protein: 32g,
Carbs: 25g, Fat: 35g**

RED MEAT AND PORK

I've teamed pork with red meat because it has every bit as much macho power! Pork doesn't have to be dry and fatty, it can be delicious with the recipes to follow. Red meat speaks for itself in the muscle-building world; a slab of steak is the image conjured in our minds when we are thinking about how to get big! In the red meat and pork chapter I will provide you with many alternative dishes to fill you up with iron, protein and much more!

BRAWNY BEEF SANDWICHES

It's a hell of a lot cheaper to make your own sandwiches and a lot healthier than the shop-bought ones too. This brawny sandwich provides plenty of protein to keep you anabolic.

Ingredients

4 slices of deli beef
4 slices of whole-wheat bread
2 tsp of mustard
Handful of baby spinach leaves
1/2 a sliced cucumber
A pinch of black pepper

How to make:

1. Get 2 slices of bread.
2. Add 2 slices of deli beef, 1 tsp of mustard, ½ a sliced cucumber, spinach and a pinch of black pepper to the slice and make a sandwich.
3. Repeat the process with the rest of the ingredients.

(Serves 1)

Calories per serving: 545, Protein: 43g, Carbs: 64g, Fat: 10g

ANABOLIC PORK SOUP

This soup is quick to prepare and full of protein to build muscle and burn fat.

Ingredients

16oz diced pork steaks
1 cup chicken stock
1 tbsp soy sauce
2 tsp Chinese five-spice powder
1 piece ginger finely chopped
1 cup of baby spinach
1 tsp of chopped red chilli,
1.5 cup of rice noodles
Handful of chopped spring onions

How to make:

1. Get a large saucepan and add all the ingredients except for the spring onions and noodles. Cover the pan and bring to a simmer on a medium heat.
2. Without letting the ingredients boil, leave to cook for around 8-10 minutes.
3. While cooking the pork, place the rice noodles in a pot of boiling water for about 5 minutes and then drain.
4. Drain and place the noodles in a bowl and add the pork and greens over the noodles. Sprinkle the spring onions over the dish and serve.

(Serves 4)

Calories per serving: 297, Protein: 21g, Carbs: 13g, Fat: 17g

POWER PORK FRUIT TRAY

This dish is absolutely delicious and one of my favourite pork recipes. Contains a good helping of protein and is low on carbs for those of you who are shredding!

Ingredients

4 pork steaks
1 tbsp olive oil
2 diced red onions
2 chopped large pears
3 sprigs of rosemary
2oz diced blue cheese
1 diced courgette
A pinch of salt and pepper
Handful of pine nuts

How to make:

1. Get a large pan and heat the olive oil on a medium heat.
2. Add the courgette, red onions, chopped pears, salt and pepper.
3. Fry for around 6 minutes until the veg starts to caramelise.
4. Pre-heat the Grill.
5. Get a cooking tray and transfer the ingredients along with the rosemary sprigs to the tray. Sprinkle some salt and pepper over the pork steaks and place them in the tray.
6. Place the tray in the oven and grill for around 10-15 minutes or until cooked right through, turning the pork steaks half way through. Add the cheese and pine nuts and let the cheese melt for a further 4-5 minutes.
7. Plate up and serve.

(Serves 4)

Calories per serving: 335, Protein: 42g, Carbs: 12g, Fat: 14g

MUSCLE BUILDING STEAK & SWEET POTATO FRIES

A great, healthy alternative to regular steak and chips! Contains a good helping of protein and slow releasing carbs.

Ingredients

4oz of sirloin steak
8oz of sweet potatoes cut into chips
1 tbsp olive oil
1 chopped red onion
1 bag of pre-washed salad
1 tbsp of balsamic vinegar
A pinch of black pepper

How to make:

1. Pre-Heat oven (375°F/190 °C/Gas Mark 5).
2. Get a baking tray, spread the chips out and bake for around 25 minutes.
3. While the chips are cooking, get a large frying pan and heat the olive oil on a medium heat.
4. Pepper the steaks and add to the pan. Fry the steaks for 6 minutes in total, turning the steaks once halfway through.
5. Take the steak and leave to cool.
6. Get a large bowl and add the salad and chopped onion. Drizzle with the vinegar and serve with the potatoes and steak.
7. the cheese and pine nuts and let the cheese melt for a further 4-5 minutes.
8. Plate up and serve.

(Serves 4)

Calories per serving: 418, Protein: 29g, Carbs: 39g, Fat: 15g

ORIENTAL BEEF MUSCLE STIR-FRY

Great beef recipe, packed with loads of protein to keep you growing and burning fat.

Ingredients

18oz of diced beef rump
1 tsp Chinese five-spice powder
2 cup of egg noodles
1 large chopped red chilli
1 chopped garlic clove
1 chopped thumb-size piece of ginger
1 stick lemongrass
2 tbsp of olive oil
4oz sugar snap peas
8 baby corns, sliced diagonally
6 chopped spring onions
½ lime
2 tbsp soy sauce
1 tbsp fish sauce
2 tbsp roasted peanuts
Handful of chopped coriander, to serve

How to make:

1. Get a bowl and add the beef and five-spice and leave to marinade. Place the egg noodles in a pot of boiling water for about 5 minutes, drain and then place to one side.
2. Mix together the chopped chilli, ginger, garlic and lemongrass in a bowl.
3. Add 1 tbsp of olive oil to a wok and heat on a medium heat. Add the ginger mixture into the wok and fry for 1 minute. Turn up the heat and add 1 more tbsp of olive oil to the wok and add the beef and fry until browned.
4. Add the sugar snaps, spring onions and baby corn to the wok and continue to stir-fry for around a minute before adding the egg noodles and mix together. Turn off the heat and add the

soy sauce, fish sauces and squeezed lime juice.
5. Place in a bowl and add the peanuts and chopped coriander to serve.

(Serves 4)

Calories per serving: 349, Protein: 34g, Carbs: 26g, Fat: 14g

BULK-UP LAMB CURRY & PEANUT STEW

This absolutely delicious curry is packed full of flavour and has a hefty dose of protein to boot.

Ingredients

1/2 cup chopped peanuts
1/2 cup canned coconut cream
4 tbsp massaman curry paste
24oz diced lamb steak (or beef)
16oz chopped white potatoes
1 chopped onion
1 cinnamon stick
1 tbsp tamarind paste
1 tbsp fish sauce
1 sliced red chilli

How to make:

1. Pre-heat oven (375°F/190 °C/Gas Mark 5).
2. Get a large casserole dish and place on the gas/electric hob on a medium heat.
3. Add 2 tbsp of coconut cream and the curry paste and fry for around a minute before adding the diced lamb. Stir in and brown. Add the rest of the coconut cream with a cup of water as well as the potatoes, onions, cinnamon stick, tamarind, fish sauce and peanuts.
4. Reduce heat to a simmer, cover the casserole, transfer to the oven and cook for 2 hours until

the lamb is soft and tender.
5. Add the sliced chilli to the top and serve.

(Serves 4)

**Calories per serving: 600, Protein: 44g,
Carbs: 38g, Fat: 46g**

MIGHTY LAMB CASSEROLE

This meal is absolutely delicious and easy to make!

Ingredients

1 tbsp of olive oil
2 cubed lamb fillets
1 chopped onion
2 chopped carrots, thickly sliced
Handful of kale
1 cup of chicken stock
1 tsp dried rosemary
1 tsp of chopped parsley
16oz of rinsed and drained cannellini beans

How to make:

1. Get a large casserole dish and heat the olive oil on a medium heat.
2. Add the lamb to the casserole dish and cook for 5 minutes until browned, then add the chopped onion and carrots. Leave to cook for another 5 minutes until the vegetables begin to soften.
3. Add the chicken stock, kale and rosemary. Then cover the casserole, leave to simmer on a low heat for 1-1.5 hours until the lamb is tender and fully cooked through.
4. Add the cannellini beans 15 minutes before the end of the cooking time.
5. Plate up and serve with the chopped parsley to garnish.

(Serves 2)

**Calories per serving: 380, Protein: 35g,
Carbs: 33g, Fat: 9g**

STEAK & CHEESE MUSCLE CLUB

Great beef recipe, packed with loads of protein to keep you growing and burning fat.

Ingredients

1 8oz sirloin steak
2 whole-meal bread rolls
1 tsp olive oil
1 tsp Dijon mustard
Handful of rocket
2oz Stilton cheese
1 tsp of balsamic vinegar
A pinch of salt and pepper

How to make:

1. Heat up a griddle pan on a high heat until very hot. Drizzle the olive oil over both sides of the steak. Sprinkle some salt and pepper over it and place the steak in the pan and fry for 3 minutes on each side. Place the steak to one side and leave to rest for a minute.
2. Cut in half to form two slices of steak.
3. Cut the whole-wheat rolls in half and place toast. Once done, add the mustard and rocket to the roll and place 1 half of the steak on top. Add balsamic vinegar and the cheese to the top and then make the sandwich.
4. Repeat steps with the other roll.

(Serves 2)

Calories per serving: 332, Protein: 32g,
Carbs: 27g, Fat: 11g

MASS GAINING LAMB FLATBREAD

A tasty and healthy homemade flatbread with a Moroccan twist, including a generous amount of protein to fuel you and your muscles!

Ingredients

2 8oz lamb leg steaks
1 tbsp harissa
4 whole meal flatbreads
4 tbsp of organic houmous
Handful of baby spinach
Handful of watercress
A pinch of salt and pepper

How to make:

1. Preheat the grill.
2. Sprinkle harissa, salt and pepper over the lamb.
3. Place lamb on a baking tray and grill for 4 minutes before turning the lamb over and cooking for a further 4 minutes. Take the tray out of the grill and leave to one side.
4. Place the flatbreads under the grill for around 1 – 2 minutes before removing and spreading on the houmous.
5. Cut the lamb into thin strips and place over the flat bread.
6. Add the baby spinach and watercress, roll the flatbread into a wrap and enjoy.

(Serves 4)

**Calories per serving: 391, Protein: 29g,
Carbs: 34g, Fat: 17g**

SUPER STEAK WITH SPICY RICE & BEANS

The perfect steak...

Ingredients

2 12oz sirloin steaks
4 tsp olive oil
1 small onion, sliced
1 cup brown long-grain rice
1½tsp fajita seasoning
1 can of drained kidney beans
Handful of chopped coriander leaves
2 tbsp tomato salsa, to serve

How to make:

1. Pour 3 tsp of oil into a deep saucepan on a medium heat and add the onion. Fry the onion for around 4 minutes.
2. Then add ½ the fajita seasoning and long grain rice. Cook for 1 minute. Add 300ml of boiling water to the saucepan and stir in. Cover the saucepan and let simmer for 20 minutes until the water has been absorbed and the rice is fluffy. Add the kidney beans and keep the pan warm.
3. While the rice is cooking, sprinkle salt and pepper over the steak as well as ½ fajita seasoning. Pre-heat a griddle pan on a high heat, add the steaks and cook for 8 minutes in total, turning the steaks half way through.
4. Add the rice to a bowl and mix in the coriander. Add a tbsp of tomato salsa to each of the steaks and serve.

(Serves 2)

Calories per serving: 650, Protein: 48g, Carbs: 60g, Fat: 26g

MUSCLE MINT LAMB STEAKS

Delicious recipe with over 40g of protein to keep you building muscle and burning fat!

Ingredients

4 8oz lamb leg steaks
2 tbsp olive oil
2 chopped garlic cloves
1 tbsp balsamic vinegar
Handful of chopped mint leaves

How to make:

1. Get a bowl and add the mint, vinegar and garlic and mix together.
2. Add the lamb to the bowl and leave to marinade for at least 30 minutes.
3. Pre-heat a griddle pan on a medium to high heat and cook the lamb for 4 minutes each side or until cooked through.
4. Serve alone or with your choice of salad for a delicious accompaniment.

(Serves 2)

Calories per serving: 367, Protein: 41g, Carbs: 2g, Fat: 22g

SUPER LAMB STEAKS WITH MEDITERRANEAN VEG

A mediterranean twist on a lamb dish! A very quick and easy, healthy lamb recipe to keep you going for longer...

Ingredients

2 8oz lamb leg/breast steaks
2 chopped courgettes
2 tbsp olive oil
Handful of rocket
2 garlic cloves, chopped
8 halved baby cherry tomatoes
Handful of chopped coriander

How to make:

1. Preheat the grill.
2. Add the oil to a pan and heat on a medium heat.
3. Throw in the courgettes, tomatoes and garlic and fry until courgettes and tomatoes are soft.
4. Add the rocket and coriander and stir in.
5. Meanwhile, sprinkle some salt and pepper over the lamb steaks. Place the lamb on a tray and grill for 4 minutes. each side.
6. Serve alongside the veg.

(Serves 2)

Calories per serving: 308, Protein: 34g, Carbs: 15g, Fat: 14g

STRENGTH AND MASS MEATLOAF

The perfect muscle building meatloaf!

Ingredients

36oz of lean ground beef
1 tsp olive oil
1 chopped red onion
1 tsp garlic
3 chopped tomatoes
1 whole beaten egg
1cup of whole wheat bread crumbs
Handful of parsley
1/4 cup of low fat parmesan
1/2 cup of organic skim milk
A pinch of salt and pepper
1 tsp oregano

How to make:

1. Preheat the oven to (400°F/200 °C/Gas Mark 6).
2. Add the oil to a pan and heat on a medium heat.
3. Cook the onions until soft but not browned. Remove the onions from the pan and let cool.
4. Get a big bowl and mix all of the ingredients together.
5. Put the meat in a big baking tray and cook on a high heat for around 30-35 minutes.
6. Serve once cooked through and piping hot.

(Serves 6)

Calories per serving: 410, Protein: 47g, Carbs: 15g, Fat: 19g

FARLEY'S MUSCLE BUILDING CHILLI CON CARNE

Who doesn't like Chilli con carne? Well this healthy version will provide you with over 30g of protein and a smug sense of satisfaction!

Ingredients

20oz lean ground beef
1 tbsp oil
1 chopped onion
1 chopped red pepper
2 crushed garlic cloves,
1 tsp of chilli powder
1 tsp paprika
1 tsp ground cumin
1 beef stock cube
16oz of tinned chopped tomatoes
2 tbsp tomato purée
16oz of dried and rinsed red kidney beans
1 cup of brown rice

How to make:

1. Get a pan and add the olive oil and heat on a medium heat.
2. Add the onions to the pan and fry until soft.
3. Then add the garlic, red pepper, chilli powder, paprika and cumin. Stir together and cook for 5 minutes.
4. Add the ground mince to the pan and cook until browned.
5. Get 300ml of hot water and add the beef stock cube to it. Add this to the pan along with the chopped tomatoes. Also add the puree and stir in well. Bring the pan to a simmer, cover and cook for around 50 minutes. Stir occasionally.
6. After 30 minutes and while the mince is cooking, add 300ml of cold water to a separate pot and heat until the water is boiling. Once boiling, add the rice and leave for 20 minutes.
7. Once the rice is done, drain and put to one side. Add the beans to the meat mix and cook for another 10 minutes.
8. Serve the rice topped with the chilli con carne.

(Serves 4)

Calories per serving: 389, Protein: 37g, Carbs: 25g, Fat: 17g

TASTY BEEF BROCCOLI STIR FRY

A very quick and easy, healthy beef stir-fry that will save you reaching out for the local Chinese delivery menu!

Ingredients

16oz of diced frying beef steaks
1 head of broccoli, broken into florets
4 chopped celery sticks
Handful of sweet corn
1 cup beef stock
2 tbsp of horseradish sauce
1 tbsp of olive oil
A pinch of salt and pepper

How to make:

1. Heat the olive oil on a medium/high heat in a frying pan.
2. Add some salt and pepper to the beefsteaks and place in the frying pan.
3. Stir-fry for 2 minutes until the beef is browned then remove and set aside.
4. Add the broccoli and chopped celery to the pan and fry for a further 2 minutes.
5. Add the beef stock to the pan, then cover. Reduce the heat and let the veg simmer for 2 minutes.
6. Place the steak back in the pan and mix with the other vegetables for another minute.
7. Plate up and serve with the horseradish sauce.

(Serves 4)

Calories per serving: 277, Protein: 30g, Carbs: 7g, Fat: 14g

BRAWN BISON BURGER

This brawny burger provides more than enough protein to keep you growing!

Ingredients

18oz of ground organic bison
3 chopped jalapeno peppers
½ chopped red onion
1 finely chopped shallot
1 egg (free range)
2 crushed garlic cloves
Sprinkle of salt and pepper

How to make:

1. Pre-heat grill to a medium heat.
2. Cover a baking tray with foil.
3. Mix all of the ingredients together in a large bowl and form palm sized patties with your hands.
4. Place your bison patties in the middle of the baking tray and slot under the grill.
5. Grill patties for around 12 – 15 minutes, turning them over halfway through.
6. Take patties out of the grill when both sides are golden and the meat is cooked through.
7. Plate and serve with a side salad.

(Serves 2)

Calories per serving: 292, Protein: 43g, Carbs: 7g, Fat: 23g

BRAWNY BEEF LETTUCE FAJITAS

Quick and easy beef recipe, perfect for lunch and packed with loads of protein to keep you growing and burning fat.

Ingredients

4oz of diced lean beef steak
1 chopped red onion
1 chopped red pepper
1 Cos or lambs lettuce, broken into whole leaves
2 tbsp of sweet chilli sauce

How to make:

1. Add the diced steak, chopped onion, red pepper and 1 tbsp of chilli sauce to a pan on a medium heat and stir-fry for around 4 – 5 minutes.
2. Add the steak mix to the whole lettuce leaves.
3. Add one more tbsp of sweet chilli sauce and roll up like a wrap.
4. Plate and serve.

(Serves 1)

Calories per serving: 329, Protein: 35g, Carbs: 33g, Fat: 6g

BULK-UP BEEF AND BROCCOLI CURRY

This absolutely delicious curry is packed full of flavour and has a hefty dose of protein to boot.

Ingredients

18oz of diced sirloin frying steak
2 tbsp of coconut oil
2 minced garlic cloves
1 tbsp of lemon juice
1.5 cup of homemade chicken stock
2 chopped carrots
1 chopped onion
2 tbsp of grated ginger
½ broccoli
Sprinkle of salt and pepper

How to make:

1. Pre-heat the coconut oil and garlic in a large pan over a medium to high heat.
2. Add the diced steak and salt to the pan and brown both sides.
3. Once brown, take the beef out and leave to one side.
4. Get a bowl and mix the pepper, ginger, lemon juice and ¼ of the homemade chicken stock.
5. Add the broccoli, onions and chopped carrots into the pan.
6. Add the last of the stock over the beef and simmer for 40 minutes or until beef soft and tender..
7. Plate and serve.

(Serves 1)

Calories per serving: 298, Protein: 30g, Carbs: 10g, Fat: 12g

PEPPERY STEAK & MUSCLE MUSHROOMS

A very quick and easy paleo meal but tasty all the same.

Ingredients

10z of rib eye steak
Sprinkle of salt and pepper
2 tbsp of olive oil
1 chopped red pepper
2 minced garlic cloves
1 cup of white baby mushrooms

How to make:

1. Get a large frying pan and heat the olive oil on a high heat.
2. Pepper the steaks and add to the pan.
3. Fry the steaks for 6 minutes in total, turning the steaks halfway through.
4. Take the steak out of the pan and leave to cool.
5. Add the baby mushrooms, peppers and cloves to the pan and sauté for around 15 minutes or until the mushrooms become soft.
6. Pour the mushroom mix over the steaks.
7. Plate and serve.

(Serves 1)

**Calories per serving: 378, Protein: 22g,
Carbs: 5g, Fat: 30g**

SUPER HERBY LAMB STEAKS

A succulent lamb dish, helping you to enjoy the taste of bulking

Ingredients

2x 8oz lamb leg steaks or equivalent weight
2 chopped zucchinis (courgettes)
2 tbsp olive oil
50g arugula (rocket)
2 garlic cloves, chopped
8 halved baby cherry tomatoes,
Handful of chopped cilantro (coriander)
Sprinkle of salt and pepper

How to make:

1. Preheat the grill to a medium to high heat.
2. Add the oil to a pan and heat on a heat.
3. Throw in the courgettes, tomatoes and garlic and fry until courgettes and tomatoes are soft.
4. Stir in the arugula and cilantro.
5. Meanwhile, sprinkle some salt and pepper over the lamb steaks.
6. Place the lamb on a baking tray and grill for 4 minutes each side.
7. Plate and serve with the roasted vegetables.

(Serves 2)

Calories per serving: 308, Protein: 34g, Carbs: 15g, Fat: 14g

PALEO BEEFY STIR FRY

A very quick and easy, healthy beef stir-fry that's packed full of protein to help you build muscle and burn fat.

Ingredients

16oz of diced frying beef steaks
1 broccoli, broken into florets
4 chopped celery sticks
1 corn on the cob (corn removed from the husk)
1 cup of organic beef or chicken stock
2 tbsp of horseradish sauce
1 tbsp of olive oil
Sprinkle of salt and pepper

How to make:

1. Heat the olive oil in a frying pan on a high heat.
2. Add salt and pepper to the beefsteaks and place them in the frying pan.
3. Stir-fry for 2 minutes until the beef is browned, then remove and set aside.
4. Add the broccoli and chopped celery to the pan and fry for a further 2 minutes.
5. Add the beef stock to the pan, then cover.
6. Reduce the heat and let the veg simmer for 2 minutes.
7. Place the steak back in the pan and mix with the other vegetables for another minute.
8. Plate and serve with the horseradish.

(Serves 4)

Calories per serving: 277, Protein: 30g, Carbs: 7g, Fat: 14g

ROASTED RUMP & ROOT VEG

Rich in iron and B vitamins - steak is a staple in the body building world. .

Ingredients

16 Oz of lean rump steak
1 Tbsp thyme
1 Tsp french mustard
1 Tbsp olive oil
1 Tsp pepper
1 Onion cut, peeled and sliced
1 Parsnip, peeled and diced
1 Rutabaga, peeled and sliced
2 Garlic cloves

How to make:

1. Preheat the oven to 450°f/250°c/Gas Mark 8.
2. Meanwhile, mix the herbs and black pepper with the mustard and olive oil.
3. Coat the rump steak and allow to marinate for as long as possible.
4. Add the rump steak to a shallow oven dish and heat the hob to a high heat. Sear each side of the beef steak for a few minutes until browned. If the baking dish is not suitable to place on the hob do this in a separate skillet first.
5. Now add the vegetables and whole garlic cloves (skin on) to the baking dish (if your beef is already in the dish make sure you use tongs to lift it first).
6. Add the dish to the oven for 25 minutes before turning the heat down to 300°f/150°c/Gas Mark 2.
7. Continue to cook for a further 8 minutes and then remove and allow to rest (the beef will continue to cook in the resting time).
8. After 5 minutes, slice the steak with a carving knife and serve on top of the juicy vegetables. The garlic should be deliciously soft by now so serve this up too!
9. Enjoy.

(Serves 2)

Calories per serving: 558, Protein: 62g, Carbs: 22g, Fat: 21g

MIX 'N' MATCH BEEF BURGER

Mix up the toppings to create your favorite burgers at home .

Ingredients

8 Oz of lean 100% grass-fed ground beef
1 Egg white
1 Tsp black pepper
1 Tsp paprika
1 Tsp mustard
2 Mini gherkins, sliced
1 Beef tomato, sliced
1/4 Cup arugula
2 Wholegrain buns

How to make:

1. Preheat the broiler to a medium high heat.
2. Mix the ground beef with the herbs, egg white, spices and mustard.
3. Use your hands to form 2 patties (about 1 inch thick).
4. Add to an oven proof baking dish and broil for 15 minutes or until meat is thoroughly cooked through. Use a knife to insert into the centre - the juices should run clear.
5. Slice your burger buns and stack with the burger, gherkin, tomato and arugula.
6. Add a little extra mustard to taste.

(Serves 2)

Calories per serving: 411, Protein: 32g, Carbs: 37g, Fat: 12g

FIT LAMB STEAKS WITH TZATZIKI

Lean lamb can still be enjoyed as a treat! .

Ingredients

2 X 5oz lean lamb steaks
1 Tbsp fresh rosemary, finely chopped
1 Tbsp extra virgin olive oil
1 Lemon, juiced
1 Tsp white wine vinegar
1/2 Cup of low fat greek yogurt
1/4 Cucumber, chopped
1/4 Cup fresh mint
1/2 Cup spinach
1 Cup couscous
1/2 Red onion, finely diced

How to make:

1. Mix the olive oil with the rosemary and marinate the lamb steaks for as long as possible.
2. Heat a skillet over a medium to high heat and add the marinated steaks, cooking for 10 minutes on each side or until thoroughly cooked through.
3. Meanwhile, add the couscous to a heatproof bowl, pour boiling water over the top, cover and leave to steam for 5 minutes.
4. Stir through the diced red pepper and 1/2 lemon juice.
5. Mix the yogurt, 1/2 lemon juice, vinegar, mint and cucumber for your tzatziki. Season with a little salt and pepper.
6. Serve the lamb steaks with the couscous and tzatziki on the side.
7. Enjoy.

(Serves 2)

Calories per serving: 403, Protein: 40g, Carbs: 25g, Fat: 15g

BODYBUILDING BEEF STEW

Stick this in the slow cooker for succulent and tender meat .

Ingredients

1 Tbsp of extra virgin olive oil
8 Oz lean beef, cubed
1 Onion, diced
4 Cups of water
1 Tsp cumin
1 Tsp turmeric
1 Tsp curry powder
1 Tsp oregano
2 Sweet potatoes, peeled and cubed
1 Red bell pepper, roughly chopped
1 Bay leaf

How to make:

1. Heat the olive oil in a skillet over a medium to high heat.
2. Add the beef and cook for 5 minutes or until browned on each side.
3. Add the vegetables and garlic to the slow cooker and pour in the water.
4. Now add the herbs, spices and bay leaf.
5. Then cover the slow cooker and cook for at least 8 hours or overnight.
6. Plate up and serve when ready to eat!

(Serves 2)

Calories per serving: 372, Protein: 25g, Carbs: 42g, Fat: 12g

MUSCLE MEATBALL & CELERIAC SPAGHETTI

Mega meaty dish with a fresh pasta.

Ingredients

8 Oz Lean Pork/Beef Mince
1 Garlic Clove, Crushed
1 Tsp Dried Thyme
2 Tbsp Extra Virgin Olive Oil
1/2 Red Onion, Finely Chopped
1 Celeriac
For The Sauce:
1 Tbsp Extra Virgin Olive Oil
1 Cup Fresh Tomatoes, Chopped (Seeds & Juices Saved)
1/4 Cup Fresh Parsley

How to make:

1. Mix the mince, 1 tbsp oil, garlic, onion and herbs in a bowl. Season with a little black pepper and separate into 8 balls, rolling with the palms of your hands.
2. Heat 1 tbsp oil in a pan over a medium heat and add the meatballs for 5 minutes or until browned.
3. Add the tomatoes, parsley (save some for garnishing) and extra olive oil.
4. Cover and lower heat to simmer for 15 minutes.
5. Meanwhile, prepare the celeriac by carefully removing any nobbly bits from the skin with a sharp knife. Use a spiralyzer to create spaghetti strips with the celeriac (place it in lengthways). If you don't have a spiralyzer you can use a potato peeler once you've cut the celeriac into quarters.
6. Add a pot of water to boil over a high heat and add the celeriac spaghetti over a steamer for 5-10 minutes or until slightly soft.
7. Drain celeriac, portion up and add meatballs and sauce over the top to serve.
8. Sprinkle with a little freshly torn basil!

(Serves 2)

Calories per serving: 374, Protein: 30g, Carbs: 35g, Fat: 26g

LEMONGRASS & CHILI BEEF

Fresh and filling..

Ingredients

1 Tbsp Coconut Oil
2X 6Oz Lean Frying Steak, Cut Into Strips
1 Stick Lemongrass,
1 Tsp Chili Flakes
1/2 Cup Sugar Snap Peas/Green Beans
1/2 Green Pepper, Sliced
1 Garlic Clove, Minced
1 Tbsp Honey
1 Cup Brown Rice
1/4 Cup Green Onions, Chopped
1 Lemon, Juiced

How to make:

1. Into a blender or pestle and mortar, add the oil, lemongrass, chili flakes, garlic and honey and blitz until nearly smooth.
2. Marinate the beef for as long as possible.
1. Heat the oil in a skillet or wok over a medium to high heat.
2. Add the beef strips and brown each side for 4 minutes.
3. Now add the green pepper and continue to cook for a further 10 minutes.
4. Add the green onions and sugar snap peas for a few more minutes.
5. Plate up and serve with brown rice and lime juice over the top.

(Serves 2)

Calories per serving: 289, Protein: 21g, Carbs: 32g, Fat: 8g

POWERFUL PORK & SPEEDY SAUERKRAUT

A German inspired meal with heaps of vitamins .

Ingredients

2X 4oz lean pork loins
1/2 White cabbage, sliced
1 Tsp salt
1 Tbsp white wine vinegar
2 Carrots, peeled and sliced
1 Tsp nutmeg

How to make:

1. Preheat the broiler to a medium high heat.
2. Sprinkle pork with nutmeg.
3. Add the pork loins to a baking tray and place under the broiler for 10-15 minutes or according to package guidelines.
4. Meanwhile, place a pot of water over a medium to high heat and add the cabbage and carrots for 5-10 minutes or until slightly softer.
5. Add the salt and vinegar to the pan.
6. Drain the cabbage and carrots and serve with the pork.
7. Enjoy!

(Serves 2)

Calories per serving: 179, Protein: 25g, Carbs: 17g, Fat: 5g

MUSCLE-FRIENDLY LASAGNE

Delicious & filling muscle building recipe .

Ingredients

10 Oz lean ground beef
1 Garlic clove, minced
1 Onion, diced
1 Tsp cayenne pepper
1 Tsp parsley
1/2 Cup canned tomatoes
1 Tsp black pepper
2 Eggplants, sliced vertically
For the white sauce:
1/4 Cup all purpose white flour
3/4 Cup rice milk
1 Tbsp ghee
1/4 Teaspoon white pepper
1 Tsp black pepper

How to make:

1. Preheat the oven to 350°f/170°c/Gas Mark 4.
2. To prepare the beef: Heat oil in a skillet on a medium to high heat and add onions and garlic for 5 minutes until soft.
3. Add lean beef mince, season with herbs and spices, add water and cook for 10-15 minutes or until completely browned.
4. Meanwhile prepare white sauce:
5. Heat saucepan on a medium heat.
6. Add the butter to the pan on the side nearest to the handle.
7. Tilt the pan towards you and allow butter to melt, whilst trying not to let it cover the rest of the pan.
8. Now add the flour to the opposite side of the pan and gradually mix the flour into the butter - continue to mix until smooth.
9. Add the milk and mix thoroughly for 10 minutes until lumps dissolve.
10. Add pepper.
11. Turn off the heat and place to one side.

12. Layer an oven proof lasagne dish with 1/3 egg-plant slices.
13. Add 1/3 beef mince on top.
14. Layer with 1/3 white sauce.
15. Repeat until ingredients are used.
16. Cover and add to the oven for 25-30 minutes or until golden and bubbly.
17. Remove and serve piping hot!

(Serves 2)

Calories per serving: 369, Protein: 31g, Carbs: 40g, Fat: 9g

BARBELL BEEF CURRY

Scrumptious beef dish.

Ingredients

1 Tsp olive oil
10 Oz lean frying beef, cut into strips
1 Onion, diced
1 Garlic clove, minced
1 Sweet potato, peeled & roughly chopped
1 Tbsp curry powder
1 Cup almond or rice milk
1 Tbsp cilantro

How to make:

1. Heat oil in a pot over a medium to high heat and sauté onions and garlic for 5 minutes or until soft.
2. Add the beef for 5-10 minutes, turning to brown each side, before adding the milk and curry powder.
3. Bring to the boil, then turn down the heat and add the sweet potato to the curry.
4. Cover and simmer for 45-50 minutes or until the beef is soft.
5. Scatter with cilantro and serve with rice.
6. Top tip: you could transfer the curry to a slow cooker and leave overnight to free you up from the stove if you wish - just ensure the liquid covers the ingredients.

(Serves 2)

Calories per serving: 418, Protein: 32g, Carbs: 32g, Fat: 18g

CHILI BEEF & MANGO SALSA

Spice things up in the kitchen.

Ingredients

1 Red onion, diced
1/2 Red bell pepper, diced
1 Garlic clove, minced
10 Oz lean ground beef
1 Red chili, finely diced
1/4 Cup kidney beans
2 Tbsp extra virgin olive oil
1/2 Cup cherry tomatoes, diced
1/4 Cup mango, diced
1/2 Lime, juiced
1 Cup quinoa
1 Tbsp fresh cilantro

How to make:

1. Bring a pan of water to the boil and add quinoa for 20 minutes.
2. Meanwhile, add 1 tbsp oil to a pan and heat on a medium to high heat.
3. Add the half the onions, pepper, chili and garlic and sauté for 5 minutes until soft.
4. Add the beef to the pan and stir until browned.
5. Now add the kidney beans and the water, cover and turn the heat down a little to simmer for 20 minutes.
6. Meanwhile, drain the water from the quinoa, add the lid and steam while the chili is cooking.
7. Prepare the salsa by mixing the rest of the onion, tomatoes, lime juice, cilantro and mango.
8. Serve chili hot with the quinoa and salsa.

(Serves 2)

Calories per serving: 591, Protein: 39g, Carbs: 51g, Fat: 27g

CHUNKY CHINESE STIR FRY

Easy to prepare and tastes delicious..

Ingredients

1 Tsp coconut oil
10 Oz lean frying beef, cut into strips
1/2 Cup green onions, diced
1 Garlic clove, minced
1 Cup whole-wheat noodles
1 Tbsp ginger, minced
1 Tsp chinese 5 spice
1/4 Cup water chestnuts
1/2 Cup broccoli florets
1 Cup coconut milk

How to make:

1. Heat oil in a wok over a high heat and sauté the beef for 5-10 minutes, turning to brown each side.
2. Add the garlic and ginger to the pan and sauté for a few minutes.
3. Now add the coconut milk, spices and water chestnuts and allow to simmer on a medium heat for 25-35 minutes or until beef is soft.
4. Meanwhile prepare noodles according to package guidelines.
5. Add the broccoli and green onions 10 minutes before serving.
6. Serve the beef over the noodles and enjoy.

(Serves 2)

Calories per serving: 433, Protein: 33g, Carbs: 26g, Fat: 21g

MOROCCAN LAMB TAGINE

Hearty, wholesome and super easy to make!.

Ingredients

1 Tbsp Of Olive Oil
2 Lean Lamb Fillets, Cubed
1 Onion, Chopped
2 Carrots,Cubed
1/2 Cup Spinach
4 Cups Of Homemade Chicken Stock
1 Tsp Dried Rosemary
1 Tsp Of Chopped Parsley
1/2 Cup Raisins
4 Tbsp Flaked Almonds

How to make:

1. In a large casserole dish, heat the olive oil on a medium high heat.
2. Add the lamb and cook for 5 minutes until browned.
3. Add the chopped onion and carrots. Leave to cook for another 5 minutes until the vegetables begin to soften.
4. Add the chicken stock, spinach, raisins and rosemary.
5. Then cover the casserole and leave to simmer on a low heat for 1-1.5 hours until the lamb is tender and fully cooked through.
6. Plate up and serve with the chopped parsley and flaked almonds to garnish.

(Serves 2)

Calories per serving: 380, Protein: 34g, Carbs: 12g, Fat: 25g

LEAN BEEF STROGANOFF

Healthy and filling.

Ingredients

1/2 Onion, diced
1 Garlic clove, minced
6 Oz lean frying beef
1 Cup low salt chicken or
Vegetable stock
1 Tsp dried oregano
1 Tbsp black pepper
1/2 Cup low fat creme fraiche
1/4 Cup whole wheat flour
2 Tbsp water
1 Cup brown rice

How to make:

1. In a crockpot or slow cooker, add the pepper, oregano, garlic, onion, stock and beef.
2. Cover and cook on high for 4-5 hours or until beef is tender.
3. Add the water, flour and creme fraiche to the crock pot and mix until smooth.
4. Continue to cook for another 20 minutes or until the mixture has thickened.
5. Meanwhile, bring a pan of water to the boil and add the rice for 20 minutes.
6. Drain the water from the rice, add the lid and steam for 5 minutes.
7. Serve the rice with the creamy beef over the top and enjoy!

(Serves 2)

Calories per serving: 382, Protein: 32g, Carbs: 44g, Fat: 12

CHILI BEEF IN LETTUCE TORTILLAS

These delicious wraps are great for lunch or dinner and are loved by the whole family! .

Ingredients

1 Garlic Clove, Minced
1/2 Cucumber, Diced
8 Oz Lean Ground Beef
1 Tbsp Chili Flakes
4 Iceberg Lettuce Leaves, Washed
1 Tsp Olive Oil

How to make:

1. Mix the ground meat with the garlic and chili flakes.
2. Heat oil in a skillet over a medium heat.
3. Add the beef to the pan and cook for 20-25 minutes or until cooked through.
4. Serve beef mixture with diced cucumber in each lettuce wrap and fold.

(Serves 2)

Calories per serving: 141, Protein: 22g, Carbs: 2g, Fat: 3g

BEEF & PEARL BARLEY CASSEROLE

Absolutely delicious.

Ingredients

2 Cups pearl barley
12Oz lean casserole beef, cubed
1 cup chicken/beef/veg stock
1 Carrot, peeled & chopped
1 Celery stalk, chopped
1 Bay leaf
1 Tbsp paprika
1 Tsp pepper
1 Tsp thyme
1 Cup white cabbage, shredded
1 Tbsp olive oil

How to make:

1. Heat the oil in a large pot over a medium to high heat and add the beef.
2. Brown each side, cooking for 6-7 minutes.
3. Now add the stock and 1 cup water along with all the rest of the ingredients.
4. Turn the heat down to a medium heat and allow to cook slowly for 1-2 hours.
5. (Alternatively you can transfer the beef and the rest of the ingredients to a slow cooker and leave to cook overnight.)
6. Serve hot and enjoy!

(Serves 4)

Calories per serving: 531, Protein: 28g, Carbs: 81g, Fat: 8g

EGGPLANT & SWEET POTATO LASAGNE

Inspired by the Greek recipe but made for body builders!

Ingredients

1 Garlic clove, minced
1 Onion, diced
8 Oz lean ground beef
1 Tsp cayenne pepper
1 Tsp thyme
1/2 Cup water
1 Tsp black pepper
1 Eggplant, sliced
1 Sweet potato, peeled & sliced
1 Cup canned tomatoes
For the cheese sauce:
1/4 Cup cottage cheese
3/4 Cup rice milk
1/4 Teaspoon white pepper
1 Tsp black pepper

How to make:

1. Preheat the oven to 350°f/170°c/Gas Mark 4.
2. To prepare cheese sauce: Whisk the cottage cheese into the rice milk until smooth. Season with the pepper and place to one side.
3. Heat oil in a skillet on a medium to high heat and add onions and garlic for 5 minutes until soft.
4. Add lean beef mince, season with herbs and spices, add tomatoes and water and cook for 10-15 minutes or until completely browned.
5. Layer an oven proof lasagne dish with 1/3 eggplant slices.
6. Add 1/3 beef mince on top.
7. Add 1/3 sweet potato slices on top.
8. Layer with 1/3 cheese sauce.
9. Repeat until ingredients are used.
10. Cover and add to the oven for 25-30 minutes or until golden and bubbly.
11. Remove and serve piping hot!

(Serves 2)

Calories per serving: 340, Protein: 30g, Carbs: 42g, Fat: 7g

STEAK, EGG & MUSHROOM FRENZY

A classic.

Ingredients

2X 8oz rump steak, sliced
4 Eggs
2 Portabello mushrooms, sliced
1 Beef tomato, sliced in half
1 Garlic clove, minced
1 Tsp peppercorns, crushed
1 Tsp chili powder
1/4 Cup green onions, chopped
1 Tbsp olive oil

How to make:

1. Mix the olive oil, chili powder and peppercorns in a shallow dish and marinade the steak for as long as possible.
2. Heat a dry skillet over a high heat.
3. When extremely hot, add the steak slices and allow to cook for 5minutes before turning over (try not to move it around the pan at all in this time).
4. Add the sliced mushroom, tomato and garlic to the pan and allow all the ingredients to sauté for a further 4 minutes.
5. Whisk the eggs with the green onions and pour over the ingredients.
6. Allow to cook like you would an omelette for 4-5 minutes or until eggs are cooked through.
7. Slide out of the skillet with a spatula.
8. Cut into 2 portions and serve.

(Serves 2)

Calories per serving: 383, Protein: 44g, Carbs: 10g, Fat: 17g

RED THAI CURRY WITH DUCK

Delicious and fresh curry with an added sweet surprise.

Ingredients

2 X duck breasts, skinless
1/2 White onion, diced
1 Red chili, diced
1 Red bell pepper, diced
2 Tbsp fresh basil leaves
1/2 Stick lemon grass, chopped
1/2 Cup coconut milk
1/2 Cup chicken stock
1 Cup cooked brown rice
1 Tbsp coconut oil
1 Garlic clove, minced

How to make:

1. Blend the chili, red pepper, basil, lemon grass and oil in a blender until a paste is formed. Alternatively use a pestle and mortar.
2. Heat a wok or skillet over a medium to high heat.
3. Spray a little cooking spray into the pan and add the duck breasts for 4 minutes on each side or until brown.
4. Add the onions and garlic and sauté for 3 minutes.
5. Now pour the coconut milk, stock and paste into the pan and stir until it dissolves.
6. Allow to simmer on a medium to low heat for 30-40 minutes or until duck is soft.
7. Add the pineapple pieces and green beans 7 minutes before serving
8. Serve with the brown rice.

(Serves 2)

Calories per serving: 373, Protein: 32g, Carbs: 31g, Fat: 15g

SLOW COOKED SPICY STEAK & BEANS

An easy dish to prepare in your slow cooker. .

Ingredients

16 Oz beef steak, diced
1/2 White onion, diced
1 Red bell pepper, diced
1 Carrot, peeled & sliced
1 Cup canned tomatoes
1/2 Cup chicken stock
2 Cup cooked brown rice
1 Garlic clove, minced
1/2 Cup black beans, canned
1 Tsp oregano
1 Tsp thyme
1 Tsp black pepper
1 Tbsp olive oil
1 Tsp curry powder

How to make:

1. Mix the olive oil with the herbs and marinade the steak for as long as possible.
2. Add to a slow cooker with the rest of the ingredients and cook overnight.
3. Serve with brown rice for a hearty meal.

(Serves 2)

Calories per serving: 394, Protein: 40g, Carbs: 37g, Fat: 10g

SWEET POTATO COTTAGE PIE

A twist on the British classic..

Ingredients

10 Oz Lean Ground Beef
1 Onion, Diced
3 Sweet Potatoes, Peeled & Sliced
1 Tbsp Greek Yogurt
1 Carrot, Peeled & Diced
1 Tsp Black Pepper
1/2 Red Bell Pepper, Diced
1 Cup Mushrooms, Sliced
1 Tsp Olive Oil
1/2 Cup Water
1 Tsp Thyme

How to make:

1. Preheat the oven to 350°f/170°c/Gas Mark 4.
2. Bring a pot of water to the boil and add the sweet potatoes.
3. Turn down the heat slightly and allow to simmer for 30 minutes.
4. Meanwhile, add oil to a pan on a medium heat.
5. Add the onions and sauté for 4-5 minutes or until soft.
6. Now add the carrots and red pepper and sauté for a further 5 minutes.
7. Add the ground beef and mix until beef is browned.
8. Add the water, turn the heat to high until it starts to bubble and then reduce the heat and add the thyme and black pepper.
9. Remove from the heat and check that the sweet potatoes are soft with a fork.
10. Drain and mash with a potato masher, adding the Greek yogurt.
11. Pour the beef mixture into a rectangular oven dish.
12. Top with the sweet potato mash.
13. Use your fork to gently score the top of the mash potato, creating soft lines along the top.
14. Add to the oven for 30-40 minutes or until golden brown.
15. Remove and serve with your choice of greens on the side.

(Serves 2)

Calories per serving: 421, Protein: 33g, Carbs: 45g, Fat: 13g

BEEF CHILI CON CARNE

A winter warmer!

Ingredients

10 Oz lean ground beef
1 Onion, diced
1/2 Cup kidney beans
1 Carrot, peeled & diced
1/2 Red bell pepper, diced
1 Cup mushrooms, sliced
1 Tsp olive oil
1/2 Cup water
1 Tbsp chili powder
1 Garlic clove, minced
1 Tsp cilantro
1 Lime
1 Cup cooked wild rice/quinoa

How to make:

1. Heat the oil in a large pot over a medium to high heat.
2. Add the onions and garlic and sauté for 5-6 minutes or until soft.
3. Add the carrot and cook for a further 5 minutes.
4. Sprinkle with chili powder.
5. Add the ground beef to the pan and stir until browned.
6. Now add the kidney beans, water and herbs.
7. Leave to cook on a medium heat for 20 minutes or until beef thoroughly cooked through.
8. Serve with a squeeze of lime juice and your choice of rice or quinoa.

(Serves 2)

**Calories per serving: 665, Protein: 43g,
Carbs: 85g, Fat: 18g**

FISH & SEAFOOD

A lot of us reserve fish for the refined. Either that or we're scared of cooking it. Fish is often easier than cooking meat; it's fresh, healthy and full of omega 3. Hopefully the recipes provided in this section will either get you started with cooking up fish, or further you down the chef road you're already on. Oh, and it will mean you burn fat, build strength, and increase brain power all at the same time!

MUSCLE MACKEREL AND SPICY COUSCOUS

Mackerel is a great healthy source of protein and is also a great source of omega-3 fats.

Ingredients

1 cup of couscous
4oz of pre cooked mackerel
1tsp of ground cumin
1 tsp of smoked paprika
1 chopped red chilli
Pinch of black pepper
2 chopped tomatoes
1 chopped onion
Handful of chopped mint

How to make:

1. Pour the couscous into a bowl and add the cumin, smoked paprika and pinch of black pepper. Then grab a cup of boiling water and pour it over the couscous until it covers it by about 1cm. Cover the bowl and leave for around 10-15 minutes.
2. When the water has been absorbed, add the chopped chilli, chopped tomatoes, chopped mint and chopped onion to the bowl and stir.
3. Add the mackerel to the top and serve.

(Serves 1)

Calories per serving: 484, Protein: 26g, Carbs: 35g, Fat: 26g

COD AND VEG

A simple recipe that's quick and easy to make and tasty too. You guessed it - high in protein and low in carbs!.

Ingredients

4oz fillet of white fish (boneless)
Handful of frozen peas
A pinch of salt and pepper
1 tbsp of olive oil
2 sliced spring onions
1 chopped gem lettuce
2 tbsp reduced-fat crème fraîche

How to make:

1. Add the lettuce, spring onions, frozen peas and olive oil to a microwave-proof bowl.
2. Season the fish with salt and pepper and 1 tbsp crème fraîche and add to the bowl.
3. Cover the bowl with cling film; pierce it several times with a fork and place in microwave.
4. Microwave the bowl for around 8 minutes until the fish as been fully cooked and is piping hot throughout.
5. Take the bowl from the microwave and remove the fish, placing to one side.
6. Use a fork to mash the vegetables and serve topped with the fish and an extra spoonful of crème fraîche.

(Serves 1)

Calories per serving: 324, Protein: 28g, Carbs: 11g, Fat: 19g

LEMONY SALMON

Salmon is a great source of protein and is very high in omega 3 fats. Most salmon dishes can be bland and boring...Not this one!.

Ingredients

4 4oz Salmon fillets
1 lemon
A pinch of salt and pepper
2 tbsp of chopped tarragon
Handful of rocket
2 tbsp of olive oil
1 chopped garlic clove

How to make:

1. Pre-Heat grill Get a bowl and add the chopped garlic, tarragon, sprinkle of salt, sprinkle of pepper and olive oil. Squeeze the lemon juice and zest in the bowl and mix everything together.
2. Add the salmon fillets to the bowl and coat them in the marinade. Cover the bowl and leave the salmon fillets to marinade for 10 minutes.
3. Take the salmon fillets out of the bowl and place on a tray, pouring the marinade over the top of the fillets.
4. Grill the salmon fillets for around 10 minutes or until cooked through.
5. Plate up and serve.

(Serves 4)

Calories per serving: 205, Protein: 20g, Carbs: 1g, Fat: 13g

STRENGTHENING SUB-CONTINENTAL SARDINES

Sardines are a great source of protein as well as omega 3's.

Ingredients

1/2 cup plain flour
10 sardines, scaled and cleaned (8 if large)
Zest of 2 whole lemons
Handful of chopped flat-leaf parsley,
3 garlic cloves, finely chopped
3 tbsp olive oil
16oz of tinned chopped tomatoes
28oz chickpeas or butterbeans, drained and rinsed
1 pack cherry tomatoes, halved
A pinch of salt and pepper

How to make:

1. Sprinkle the flour with salt and pepper and spread the flour out on the work surface.
2. Cover the sardines with the flour on each side.
3. Now in a separate bowl add the lemon zest to the chopped parsley (save a pinch for garnishing) and half of the chopped garlic, ready for later.
4. Put a very large pan on the grill and heat on high.
5. Now add the oil and once very hot, lay the floured sardines flat.
6. Fry for 3 minutes until golden underneath and turn over to fry for another 3 minutes. Put these onto a plate to rest.
7. Fry the remaining garlic (add another splash of oil if you need to) for 1 min until softened. Pour in the tin of chopped tomatoes, mix and let simmer for 4-5 minutes.
8. Tip in the chickpeas or butter beans and fresh tomatoes, then stir until heated through.

9. Here's when you add the sardines into the lemon and parsley mix and cook for a further 3-4 minutes.
10. Once they're cooked through, serve with a pinch of parsley to garnish.

(Serves 4)

Calories per serving: 356, Protein: 20g, Carbs: 52g, Fat: 7g

MUSCLE BUILDING SARDINES ON TOAST

A quick and easy muscle-building recipe to make: perfect for lunches or snacks.

Ingredients

4 slices Ezekiel bread or whole wheat brown bread
2 cans of drained sardines in olive oil
1 tbsp olive oil
1 chopped garlic clove
1 chopped red chilli
1 lemon, zest and juice
Handful of chopped parsley

How to make:

1. Toast the bread.
2. Heat some olive oil in a pan on a medium heat.
3. Add the chilli, garlic, lemon zest and sardines and heat for 2-3 minutes until cooked.
4. Place the sardines on the toast and sprinkle the parsley over them. Finish off with a few drops of lemon juice to serve.

(Serves 2)

Calories per serving: 442, Protein: 24g, Carbs: 30g, Fat: 23g

MIGHTY TUNA MELTS

Not sure what to do with that tuna can at the back of the cupboard? This is a delicious protein packed recipe that's ready in minutes.

Ingredients

8oz of tinned, drained tuna
2 chopped spring onions stems
4 tbsp low-fat mayonnaise
4 thick slices Ezekial or wholemeal bread
1/2 cup grated low fat cheddar
2 tbsp of chilli flakes
1 squeezed lemon
A pinch of salt and pepper

How to make:

1. Toast the bread and pre-heat the grill.
2. Get a bowl and add the spring onions, mayonnaise, tuna and chilli flakes along with salt and pepper and the lemon juice. Mix everything together.
3. Spread the tuna mix over the top of the slices of bread and sprinkle the grated cheese over the top. Place under the grill until the cheese starts to bubble.
4. Plate up and serve.

(Serves 2)

Calories per serving: 450, Protein: 37g, Carbs: 20g, Fat: 24g

TASTY TUNA, BROCCOLI & CAULIFLOWER PASTA BAKE

Delicious pasta meal packed with protein for all your muscle-building and fat loss needs.

Ingredients

2 cans of tuna in olive oil (drained)
28oz of canned chopped tomatoes
2 cups whole-wheat pasta
8oz chopped broccoli
8oz chopped cauliflower
8oz pack light soft cheese
4oz of grated cheddar
1/4 cup whole-wheat breadcrumbs
1 tbsp of olive oil

How to make:

1. Grab a pan and heat the olive oil (medium/high heat).
2. Add the canned tomatoes and 200ml of water and let simmer.
3. Heat another large pan of water until it boils. Add the whole-wheat pasta and leave until the pan starts to boil again. Reduce the heat until the water simmers. Leave the whole-wheat pasta to cook for around 10 minutes. Add the broccoli and cauliflower during the last 3 minutes then drain.
4. Whilst the pasta and veg is cooking, pre heat the grill.
5. Add the cheese to the tomato sauce and stir until it melts, then add the drained pasta, vegetables and tuna.

6. Pour the mixture in a deep tray and cover with the cheddar, breadcrumbs, salt and pepper.
7. Place under the grill and cook for 6 minutes until golden.
8. Plate up and serve.

(Serves 4)

Calories per serving: 641, Protein: 37g, Carbs: 73g, Fat: 22g

SUPER HUMAN SEA BASS WITH SIZZLING SPICES

A delicious meaty meal that's packed full of protein.

Ingredients

6 x sea bass fillets skin on and scaled
3 tbsp olive oil
1 thumb-size piece of ginger, peeled and chopped into slices
3 thinly sliced garlic cloves
3 red chillies deseeded and thinly sliced
5 sliced spring onion stems
1 tbsp soy sauce

How to make:

1. Get a large pan and heat 2 tbsp of the oil on a medium heat.
2. Sprinkle salt and pepper over the Sea Bass and score the skin of the fish a few times with a sharp knife.
3. Add the sea bass fillet to the very hot pan with the skin side down (you must press the fish down onto the pan with your cooking spatula to prevent the fish from shrivelling and shrinking).
4. Cook the fish this way for around 5 minutes, or until you can see the skin underneath turning golden brown (you can lose the pressure on the spatula after the first few seconds)!
5. Now turn the fish over for around 30 seconds to give the flesh a nice golden colour.
6. Take the fish out of the pan, and place to one side.
7. Add the rest of the oil to the pan, throw in the chillies, garlic and ginger and cook for approximately 2 minutes or until golden.
8. Take this off the heat and add the spring onions with the soy sauce. Pour the sauce over your sea bass for a delicious oriental treat.

(Serves 6)

Calories per serving: 202, Protein: 28g, Carbs: 2g, Fat: 9g

PROTEIN PACKED PAELLA

A delicious, traditional Spanish dish that's packed full over flavour and protein to ensure you continue to build muscle and burn fat.

Ingredients

8oz frozen cooked prawns
2 diced chorizo sausages
1 tbsp olive oil
1 chopped onion
1 chopped garlic clove
½ tsp turmeric
3 cups cooked brown rice
1 cups frozen peas

How to make:

1. Heat olive oil in a pan on a high heat. Add the chorizo, onion and garlic and then fry for 2-3 minutes until soft.
2. Add the turmeric, rice, prawns and frozen peas as well as 1 cup of boiling water.
3. Stir until everything is warm and the water has been absorbed.
4. Plate up and serve.

(Serves 4)

Calories per serving: 351, Protein: 21g, Carbs: 50g, Fat: 9g

BRAWNY BAKED HADDOCK WITH SPINACH AND PEA RISOTTO

Haddock is cheap and easy to cook and on top of this is packed full of nutrients and is a warm and wholesome filler

Ingredients

16oz skinless, boneless, smoked haddock from your local fishmonger or supermarket
1 tbsp olive oil
1 onion, chopped
2 cups risotto rice
2cups of vegetable stock
2 cups fresh spinach leaves
Handful of frozen peas
3 tbsp crème fraîche
1/4 cup grated parmesan cheese
A pinch of pepper

How to make:

1. Heat the oil in a large pan or wok on a medium heat.
2. Fry the chopped onion until just soft (not brown) before adding in the rice and stirring until soft.
3. Now add half of the stock and continue to stir slowly until the rice takes on a translucent texture.
4. Keep adding the rest of the stock slowly whilst stirring for up to 20-30 minutes.
5. Stir in the spinach and peas to the risotto.
6. Place the fish on top of the rice, replace the lid, then let steam for 10 minutes.
7. Flake the fish into large chunks and stir into the rice with the crème fraîche and half the parmesan.

8. Sprinkle with freshly ground pepper, then add the rest of the parmesan on top to taste!

(Serves 4)

Calories per serving: 469, Protein: 32g, Carbs: 66g, Fat: 10g

RUSTIC SCALLOPS WITH CORIANDER AND LIME

Scallops are a delicacy and if you feel like pushing the boat out, a great tasty change from the norm!

Ingredients

8 queen or king scallops (row on)
1 tbsp olive oil
2 large chopped garlic cloves
1 tsp chopped fresh red chilli
1/2 lime juice
2 tbsp of chopped coriander
A pinch of salt and pepper

How to make:

1. Heat pan on a medium to high and fry scallops for about 1 minute each side until golden. Add the chopped chilli and garlic cloves to the pan and squeeze the lime juice over the scallops.
2. Remove the scallops and sprinkle the chilli and coriander over them as well as some salt and pepper to serve.

(Serves 4)

Calories per serving: 225, Protein: 20g, Carbs: 3g, Fat: 14g

TRAINING TILAPIA IN THAI SAUCE

Tilapia is an exotic sounding fish but can often be found in your local fishmonger or superstore counter. Failing this, you can use this recipe with Sea Bass or any other fish fillets of your choice!

Ingredients

4 tilapia fillets
2 tbsp flour
2 tbsp olive oil
4 spring onion stems, sliced
1 stick of chopped lemon grass
2 crushed garlic cloves
1 thumb-size piece of chopped fresh ginger
2 tbsp soy sauce
Lime juice of 1 lime, plus 1 lime chopped into wedges, to serve
1 chopped red chilli
Handful of coriander leaves

How to make:

1. Dip the tilapia fillets into the flour so that the whole fillet is coated.
2. Add olive oil to a pan on a medium to high heat and fry the fillets for 3 minutes on each side.
3. Using the same pan, fry the garlic, chilli, lemon grass and ginger on a low heat, adding the soy sauce and lime juice and simmering until the sauce thickens slightly.
4. Spoon the sauce over the fish and add the spring onions for a couple of minutes before dishing up and garnishing with your choice of herb and the lime wedges on the side.

(Serves 4)

Calories per serving: 328, Protein: 28g, Carbs: 25g, Fat: 14g

TANGY TROUT

Trout is the king of all river fish and its good-ness cannot be underrated! Sea trout is just as majestic so don't rule it out!

Ingredients

4 trout fillets
1/4 cup whole wheat/brown breadcrumbs (you can buy these pre-packaged or just use your trusty blend-er to wiz up your crust ends!)
1 tbsp olive oil
1 small chopped bunch parsley
Zest and juice of 1 lemon
1/4 cup toasted and chopped pine nuts or walnuts

How to make:

1. Turn your grill up high.
2. In the meantime, spread a little oil over a baking tray and mix the breadcrumbs, parsley, lemon zest and juice and half of the nuts.
3. Lay the fillets skin side down onto your tray and rub into your mixture on both sides before driz-zling with more olive oil.
4. Leave them under the grill for five minutes and then scatter over the rest of the nuts to serve.

(Serves 4)

Calories per serving: 298, Protein: 30g, Carbs: 10g, Fat: 16g

STEAMY WORKOUT FISH

This dish is fresh and delicious; it's so easy to cook and you can pack it full with extra greens and vitamins!

Ingredients

Tin foil, greaseproof paper or baking paper.
4 oz pak choi
4 x 8oz fillets firm white fish (Cod, Plaice, Pollock, Seabass or Haddock)
2 garlic cloves, finely chopped
2 tbsp soy sauce
1 tsp mirin rice wine
4 chopped spring onions stems
Handful of chopped coriander

How to make:

1. Heat oven to (200°C/400°F/Gas Mark 6).
2. You're going to be making a parcel for your delicious ingredients so you will need tin foil, greaseproof paper or baking paper.
3. Cut off four large rectangles and place each fillet on each piece of paper.
4. Add the garlic, soy sauce and rice wine.
5. You may want to use one or two of the lime wedges to squeeze the juices into your parcel.
6. Fold these up into a parcel leaving one edge open.
7. Cook for 20 minutes then add the spring onions and chilli for a fresh taste to end.

(Serves 4)

Calories per serving: 145, Protein: 29g, Carbs: 4g, Fat: 1g

JOCK'S JACKET POTATO WITH TUNA

Who said a jacket potato had to be boring? Try this sweet potato version and you'll be left satisfied and full with your fair share of protein!

Ingredients

1 large sweet potato
6oz can tuna in olive oil, drained
½ finely chopped red onion,
1 small deseeded and chopped red chilli, (dried chilli will be just as good)
1 tbsp natural yoghurt
A bunch of chopped spring onions

How to make:

1. Preheat the oven to (200°C/400°F/Gas Mark 6).
2. You don't need to peel the sweet potato but you may want to scrape off the nobly bits with a sharp knife!
3. Pierce the potato with a fork multiple times and place in the microwave for 20 minutes (if you don't have a microwave you can use the oven but it will take around 30 minutes).
4. Whilst it's cooking, mix the tuna with the chopped onion and chill and season with salt and pepper.
5. Place the sweet potato in the pre-heated oven for a further 5-10 minutes or until a little crispy and serve with the tuna mix and yoghurt over the top.
6. Sprinkle the chopped spring onion over that

(Serves 4)

Calories per serving: 352, Protein: 33g, Carbs: 27g, Fat: 13g

SUPER COD PARCELS

A simple recipe that's quick and easy to make and tasty too.

Ingredients

2x 6oz cod fillets
2 sheets of grease-proof or baking paper
2 tbsp chopped flat-leaf parsley
Juice of 1 lemon
1 cup organic cherry tomatoes
25g olives
1 tbsp olive oil

How to make:

1. Preheat oven to (180°C /350°f/Gas Mark 4).
2. Tear off a square of paper and place a cod fillet in the centre.
3. Scatter half of the other ingredients around it and fold shut.
4. Repeat with the other cod fillet.
5. Bake for 15 minutes in the oven.
6. Open the parcel and squeeze more lemon juice over to serve.
7. Plate and serve.

(Serves 1)

Calories per serving: 324, Protein: 28g, Carbs: 11g, Fat: 19g

TANGY SEABASS & TENDER-STEM BROCCOLI

A healthy duo to boost brainpower and strength - essential for a perfect workout.

Ingredients

2x 4oz sea bass fillets (skin on)
1 bunch of tender stem broccoli (or half a head of broccoli)
2 tbsp olive oil
Juice of 1 lime
Sprinkle of salt and pepper

How to make:

1. Place a pan of water on a high heat and leave to boil.
2. Add the broccoli into the boiling water for 5-6 minutes.
3. Heat the oil in a separate pan on a medium heat and place the sea bass, skin down on to the pan. Hold the fillet for a few seconds to prevent the sides from curling up and shrinking.
4. Cook for 3 minutes and turn over.
5. Take the broccoli off the heat, drain and put to one side (check for taste first– crunchy is best but some like it softer!)
6. Cook the sea bass fillets for a further 2-3 minutes.
7. Add the lime juice to the sea bass and salt and pepper to taste.
8. Plate and serve the sea bass with the broccoli.

(Serves 2)

Calories per serving: 223, Protein: 20g, Carbs: 5g, Fat: 15g

BRIT FISH AND CHIPS

A winter warmer served with chips that you're actually allowed to indulge in.

Ingredients

2 large sweet potatoes, peeled and cut into thick chips (fries)
3 tbsp olive oil
1 garlic clove, crushed
Juice of 1 lemon
2x 4oz skinless white fish fillets (look for sustainably caught)
A serving of fresh green peas
Handful of finely chopped fresh mint
Sprinkle of salt and pepper

How to make:

1. Heat oven to (180°C /400°f/Gas Mark 6).
2. Boil a pan of water on a high heat.
3. Place the sweet potato fries in the pan of boiling water and leave for 10 minutes.
4. Drain the sweet potatoes (keep the water but turn the pan off!) and spread out on an oven dish.
5. Drizzle the sweet potatoes with ½ the olive oil and salt and pepper and place in the oven.
6. Cook the sweet potato for 15 minutes before adding the fish fillets to the dish, sprinkling with the rest of the olive oil and salt and pepper.
7. Allow the fish fillets to cook for 10-15 minutes or to the recommended guidelines on the packaging.
8. A few minutes before the fish is ready, place the peas into the pan of water and allow to boil on a high heat.
9. Drain the peas and add the mint.
10. Stir with half the squeezed lemon.
11. Remove the fish and chips from the oven before squeezing the rest of the lemon over the fish.

12. A last sprinkle of salt and pepper to taste.
13. Plate and serve and enjoy your British classic the paleo way

(Serves 2)

Calories per serving: 385, Protein: 25g, Carbs: 25g, Fat: 24g

LANGOUSTINE AND RED PEPPER RICE-FREE PAELLA

A Mediterranean Masterpiece

Ingredients

3 tbsp olive oil
2 red peppers, cut into cubes (about ½ cm thick)
Handful of black olives
1 zucchini (courgette) cut into cubes about ½ cm thick
1 tbsp paprika
7 large organic tomatoes cut into eight pieces
12oz langoustines - butterflied
1 fresh lemon, cut into quarters
1 serving of cooked fresh peas

How to make:

1. Heat oven to (150°C /300°f/Gas Mark 2).
2. Oil a baking tray and add the tomatoes, pepper, olives and zucchini.
3. Drizzle a little more olive oil over the vegetables and sprinkle salt and pepper and paprika over the top.
4. Oven bake for 30-40 minutes.
5. Whilst your vegetable mix is roasting, butterfly your langoustines:
6. Pull off the head and legs with your fingers and leave the tails for presentation.
7. Score down the centre of each prawn (do not slice in half) and then pull open on each side of the score to flatten.
8. Turn the oven up to (180°C /350°f/Gas Mark 4) and add your prawns to a roasting tray, drizzle with olive oil.
9. Cook for 6-7 minutes, ensuring piping hot before serving.
10. Serve the roasted vegetables (with added peas) in a pasta/rice dish with the prawns on top and the lemon wedges for squeezing.
11. Add salt and pepper to taste.

(Serves 2)

Calories per serving: 353, Protein: 40g, Carbs: 22g, Fat: 25g

SUPER HUMAN MACKEREL & BRAWNY BEETROOT

A delicious mackerel meal - packed full of protein and super-charged beetroot.

Ingredients

8oz skinned sweet potatoes
8oz smoked mackerel fillets, skin removed
4 spring onions, finely sliced
6oz small cooked beetroot, sliced into wedges
Small bunch dill, finely chopped
1 tsp caraway seeds
2 tbsp olive oil
Juice 1 lemon, zest of half

How to make:

1. Place a pan of water on a high heat and leave to boil.
2. Add the broccoli into the boiling water for 5-6 minutes.
3. Heat the oil in a separate pan on a medium heat and place the sea bass, skin down on to the pan. Hold the fillet for a few seconds to prevent the sides from curling up and shrinking.
4. Cook for 3 minutes and turn over.
5. Take the broccoli off the heat, drain and put to one side (check for taste first– crunchy is best but some like it softer!)
6. Cook the sea bass fillets for a further 2-3 minutes.
7. Add the lime juice to the sea bass and salt and pepper to taste.
8. Plate and serve the sea bass with the broccoli.

(Serves 2)

Calories per serving: 223, Protein: 20g, Carbs: 5g, Fat: 15g

CATCH OF THE DAY

A wild and fresh treat..

Ingredients

1 whole trout cleaned and gutted (best caught yourself! If fishing doesn't come naturally, make sure it's sustainable)
2 green peppers, deseeded and chopped
8 cherry tomatoes halved
Handful of cilantro (coriander)
Handful of parsley
1 fresh lemon
1 clove minced garlic
1 tbsp olive oil,
Sprinkle of salt and pepper

How to make:

1. Heat oven to (190°C /375°f/Gas Mark 5).
2. Stuff the trout with the fresh herbs (save a handful for garnish), olive oil, and garlic.
3. Add to an oiled baking tray, surrounded by the vegetables.
4. Cook for 10-15 minutes – the fish must be piping hot before serving.
5. Serve with the lemon chunks and garnish with a handful of leftover herbs.

(Serves 1)

Calories per serving: 504, Protein: 36g, Carbs: 17g, Fat: 33g

SUPER STRONG SALMON FRITTATA

(Serves 4)

Calories per serving: 340, Protein: 25g, Carbs: 15g, Fat: 20g

A tasty paleo meal that will keep you building muscle and burning fat!

Ingredients

2x 5oz wild salmon fillets
1 head of broccoli (pull off the florets)
1 tbsp olive oil
Handful of cilantro (coriander) and parsley
8 free range eggs, beaten
2 large peeled, sweet potatoes.

How to make:

1. Bring a pan of water to the boil on a high heat and add the sweet potatoes, cook for 20 minutes.
2. Steam the salmon over the pan for the last 15 minutes.
3. Add the broccoli in the same pan as the potatoes for the last 4-5 minutes of cooking and then drain.
4. Use your fork to flake the cooked salmon into a separate bowl whilst the potatoes and broccoli are cooling.
5. Use a knife to roughly chop the sweet potato into thin slices.
6. Mix the broccoli, sweet potato and salmon.
7. Heat the olive oil in a pan on a medium heat.
8. Add the potato and broccoli and salmon in a large omelette shape.
9. Mix eggs with herbs and pour over the ingredients.
10. Cook on a medium heat for 6-7 minutes (once edges are brown and a little crispy use a flat spatula to lift from the base of the pan and prevent sticking).
11. Continue to cook on a low heat for a further 5 minutes or until frittata can be easily lifted from the pan with your spatula.
12. Serve on a bed of salad!

TRAINING THAI BROTH

An Asian take on bodybuilding feasts.

Ingredients

2x 5oz skinless cod pieces
2 tbsp olive oil
1 tbsp coriander seeds
2 fresh limes
1 garlic clove
1 thumb size piece of minced ginger
1 white onion, chopped
1/4 cup spinach leaves
Handful of fresh basil leaves
1 pak choi
1 cup of homemade chicken stock
1 cup of good quality organic coconut milk (if available)
1 small green pepper deseeded and finely chopped
2 stems of spring onion, chopped

How to make:

1. Crush the fresh herbs and spices in a blender or use a pestle and mortar.
2. Mix in to 1 tbsp of olive oil until a paste is formed.
3. Heat a large pan or wok with sesame oil on a high heat.
4. Fry the onions, garlic and ginger until soft but not crispy or browned.
5. Add the spice paste with the coconut milk and stir.
6. Slowly add the stock until a broth is formed.
7. Now add your fish pieces and allow to simmer in the broth for 10-15 minutes.
8. Add the pak choi leaves 2-3 minutes before the end of the cooking time.
9. Plate and serve hot with the chilli and spring onion sprinkled over the top.

(Serves 2)

Calories per serving: 440, Protein: 40g, Carbs: 25g, Fat: 20g

STEAMY PALEO WORKOUT FISH

This dish is fresh and delicious; it's so easy to cook and you can cram it full with extra greens and vitamins!.

Ingredients

2x 6oz trout fillets
4 rectangles of tin foil or baking paper
1 large red pepper, deseeded and chopped
2 large tomatoes, roughly chopped
1 garlic clove, chopped
1 tbsp olive oil, plus a little extra
1 tbsp balsamic vinegar
2 tbsp flaked almonds
1/4 arugula (rocket)
1 lime cut into wedges

How to make:

1. Heat oven to (200°C /400°f/Gas Mark 6).
2. Cut off four large rectangles and place each fillet on each piece of paper.
3. Mix the balsamic vinegar, ½ lime juice, red pepper, tomatoes, garlic, almonds and olive oil in a separate bowl.
4. Drizzle generously over each trout fillet.
5. Fold these up into a parcel leaving one edge open.
6. Cook for 20 minutes then add the spring onions and chilli for a fresh taste to end.
7. Plate and serve with the remaining lime wedges.

(Serves 2)

Calories per serving: 208, Protein: 20g, Carbs: 5g, Fat: 12g

CALAMARI & SHRIMP PAELLA

Mouthwatering!

Ingredients

6 Oz frozen cooked shrimp
1 Cup calamari, fresh or frozen
1 Tbsp olive oil
1 Red onion, chopped
1 Garlic clove, chopped
1 Tsp paprika
1 Tsp chili flakes
1 Tbsp oregano
1 Cup cooked brown rice
1/2 Cup frozen peas

How to make:

1. Heat olive oil in a pan on a medium to high heat.
2. Add the onion and garlic and then fry for 2-3 minutes until soft.
3. Add the calamari and sauté for 5-10 minutes or until hot through.
4. Now add the shrimp and sauté for a further 5 minutes or until hot through.
5. Now add the herbs and spices, rice and frozen peas with 1/2 cup boiling water.
6. Stir until everything is warm and the water has been absorbed.
7. Plate up and serve.

(Serves 2)

Calories per serving: 313, Protein: 27g, Carbs: 33g, Fat: 11g

SALMON FILLET & PESTO MASH

Add a little twist to your normal salmon dish

Ingredients

2X salmon fillets
1 Tsp black pepper
1 Tbsp extra virgin olive oil
2 Sweet potatoes, peeled and cubed
For the pesto:
1/2 Cup fresh basil
1/2 Cup fresh spinach
1 Tsp black pepper
1/4 Cup extra virgin olive oil
1 Garlic clove, minced

How to make:

1. Prepare the pesto by blending all the ingredients for the pesto in a food processor or grinding with a pestle and mortar. Place to one side.
2. Boil a pan of water on a high heat and add the sweet potatoes.
3. Allow to boil for 20-25 minutes or until very soft.
4. Drain and use a potato masher to mash the sweet potatoes.
5. Fold the pesto through the mash.
6. Now grab a skillet and heat the oil over a medium to high heat.
7. Sprinkle black pepper over the salmon fillets and score the skin of the fish a few times with a sharp knife.
8. Add the fish to the very hot pan with the skin side down.
9. Cook for 7-8 minutes and turn over (this will allow the skin to turn crispy and golden).
10. Cook for a further 3-4 minutes or until cooked through.
11. Remove fillets from the skillet and allow to rest.
12. Serve with the pesto mash and a side of greens.

(Serves 2)
Calories per serving: 506, Protein: 28g, Carbs: 22g, Fat: 35g

FENNEL & OLIVE SEA BASS

Fuel up with this tasty fish dish!

Ingredients

2X sea bass fillets
1 Tsp black pepper
1 Tsp extra virgin olive oil
1 Fennel bulb, sliced
1 Garlic clove
1/4 Cup olives
2 Green onion stems, sliced
1 Lemon
1 Cup couscous

How to make:

1. Preheat the oven to 375°f/190°c/Gas Mark 5.
2. Sprinkle black pepper over the Sea Bass and score the skin of the fish a few times with a sharp knife.
3. Slice the fennel bulb and garlic clove.
4. Tear off two squares of baking paper or tin foil and add half of the fennel bulb, garlic, olives and green onions stems to the centre of the paper.
5. Place the sea bass fillet on top squeeze half the lemon juice in each parcel.
6. Add the rest of the lemon to each parcel.
7. Fold up loosely and add to the oven for 12-15 minutes or until fish is thoroughly cooked through and flakes easily.
8. Meanwhile, add boiling water to your couscous, cover and allow to steam.
9. Once it has soaked up the water, use your fork to fluff the couscous.
10. Add a little salt and pepper and olive oil and then serve the sea bass, vegetables and all the lovely juices from the parcel over the couscous.

(Serves 2)

Calories per serving: 278, Protein: 25g, Carbs: 23g, Fat: 9g

BULK-UP SARDINES WITH LEMON, GARLIC & PARSLEY

European inspired sardines.

Ingredients

8 Oz sardines, fresh or canned
1 Tsp black pepper
1 Tbsp extra virgin olive oil
1 Lemon, juiced
1/4 Cup wild garlic (or 2 garlic cloves)
1/4 Cup fresh parsley, chopped

How to make:

1. Mix the olive oil, pepper, parsley and garlic in a bowl.
2. Marinate the sardines in the mixture for as long as possible.
3. When ready to cook, preheat the broiler to a medium heat.
4. Add the sardines to a lined baking dish and place under the broiler for 8-12 minutes or until thoroughly cooked through.
5. Enjoy!

(Serves 2)

Calories per serving: 215, Protein: 20g, Carbs: 1g, Fat: 14g

COD, PEA &
SPINACH RISOTTO

A healthy yet delicious risotto dish.

Ingredients

2X smoked cod fillets skinless, boneless
1 Tbsp extra virgin olive oil
1 White onion, finely diced
2 Cups brown rice
4 Cups vegetable stock
1 Cup fresh spinach leaves
1 Cup of frozen peas
3 Tbsp low fat greek yogurt (optional)
A pinch of black pepper
4 Lemon wedges
1 Cup of arugula

How to make:

1. Heat the oil in a large pan on a medium heat.
2. Sauté the chopped onion for 5 minutes until soft before adding in the rice and
3. stirring for 1-2 minutes.
4. Add half of the stock and stir slowly.
5. Slowly add the rest of the stock whilst continuously stirring for up to 20-30 minutes (this is a bit of a workout!)
6. Stir in the spinach and peas to the risotto.
7. Place the fish on top of the rice, cover and steam for 10 minutes.
8. Use your fork to break up the fish fillets and stir into the rice with the yogurt.
9. Sprinkle with freshly ground pepper to serve and a squeeze of fresh lemon.
10. Garnish with the lemon wedges and serve with the arugula.

(Serves 2)

Calories per serving: 527, Protein: 34g, Carbs: 74g, Fat: 12g

RAINBOW TROUT

Multiply your reps with this dish!.

Ingredients

1 Whole trout, gutted by your fishmonger
1/4 Red pepper, diced
1/4 Yellow pepper, diced
1/4 Green pepper, diced
1 Lime, juiced
1/4 Cup cooked couscous
1 Tsp thyme
1 Tsp oregano
1 Tsp black pepper
1 Tbsp extra virgin olive oil

How to make:

1. Preheat the broiler on a high heat.
2. Lightly oil a baking tray.
3. Mix all of the ingredients apart from the trout and lime.
4. Slice the trout lengthways (there should be an opening here from where it was gutted) and stuff the mixed ingredients inside.
5. Squeeze the lime juice over the fish and then place the lime wedges on the tray.
6. Place under the broiler on the baking tray and broil for 15-20 minutes or until fish is thoroughly cooked through and flakes easily.
7. Enjoy with a salad of your choice.

(Serves 1)

Calories per serving: 330, Protein: 20g, Carbs: 20g, Fat: 19g

LANGOUSTINE & SWEET POTATO FRIES

Posh body building grub!

Ingredients

For the fries:
2 Large sweet potatoes, cut into fries
1 Tsp of cumin
1 Tbsp of extra virgin olive oil
1/2 Tsp of black pepper
1/2 Tsp of paprika
1 Dash of cayenne pepper
For the langoustine:
2 Cups of whole langoustines
1 Tbsp ghee
1 Tbsp fresh parsley
1 Lemon

How to make:

1. Preheat oven to 375°F/190 °C/Gas Mark 5.
2. Add the sweet potato strips into a large bowl.
3. Drizzle with some olive oil.
4. Sprinkle the rest of the ingredients over the top.
5. Toss together gently to evenly coat the potatoes.
6. Get a baking sheet and arrange the coated potatoes into a thin layer.
7. Bake for around 30 minutes or until cooked through.
8. Meanwhile, prepare your langoustines by boiling a pan of water non a high heat and boiling langoustines for 5 minutes.
9. Remove from heat and chop the langoustines in half (lengthways). Remove the vein from the middle with a sharp knife.
10. Mix the ghee, parsley and lemon.
11. Heat a skillet on a medium to high heat and add the langoustine before drizzling the parsley and ghee over the top and leave to cook for 10 minutes or until cooked through. Serve with the sweet potato fries!

(Serves 2)

Calories per serving: 357, Protein: 13g, Carbs: 22g, Fat: 14g

TOMATO & WALNUT SOLE

The crunchy topping on this fish makes it stand out from the crowd and the kale is rich in vitamins and iron.

Ingredients

2 Tsp extra virgin olive oil
1/2 Cup walnuts
1 Egg white
2X sole fillets, skinless
2 Tsp whole grain mustard
1 Head of kale, chopped
1 Clove of garlic, mashed
1 Cup canned chopped tomatoes,

How to make:

1. Preheat oven to 350°f/170°c/Gas Mark 4.
2. Lightly oil a baking sheet with 1 tsp extra virgin olive oil.
3. Mix the walnuts and egg white together.
4. Spread a thin layer of the mustard over the fish and then dip into the walnut mixture.
5. Transfer to baking dish.
6. Bake for 12 minutes or until cooked through.
7. Meanwhile, heat 1 tsp oil in a skillet on a medium heat and sauté the garlic for 30 seconds, adding in the tomatoes and kale for a further 5 minutes.
8. Serve the fish with the tomato sauce over the top

(Serves 2)

Calories per serving: 492, Protein: 30g, Carbs: 16g, Fat: 36g

SALMON BURGERS WITH AVOCADO

Salmon burgers are delicious and packed with healthy oils and fats.

Ingredients

1 Beaten free range egg
2 Cans of wild salmon, drained
2 Scallions, chopped
2 Tbsp coconut oil
1 Tsp dill, chopped
1 Avocado
1 Lime
1 Cup cooked brown rice
1 Cup spinach, washed

How to make:

1. Combine the salmon, egg, dill, scallions and 1 tbsp oil in a bowl, mixing well with your hands to form 2 patties.
2. Heat 1 tbsp oil over a medium heat in a skillet and cook the patties for 4 minutes each side until firm and browned.
3. Squeeze the lime juice over the top and flip once more.
4. Peel and slice the avocado.
5. Stack the burgers with the avocado sliced on top and a helping of spinach leaves and serve brown rice.

(Serves 2)

Calories per serving: 611, Protein: 62g, Carbs: 34g, Fat: 34g

HEAVY HADDOCK & BEAN STEW

A great warm up.

Ingredients

2X haddock fillets
A pinch of black pepper
1 Cup homemade chicken broth
1 Cup canned tomatoes
1 Tsp olive oil
1 Carrot, diced
2 Tsp cilantro, finely chopped
1/4 Cup turkey bacon
1/2 Cup chickpeas
1 Tsp parsley
1 Tsp cilantro

How to make:

1. Rub the fish with pepper.
2. In a large saucepan, heat the oil on a medium heat and cook the carrot and turkey bacon for 5 minutes.
3. Add the chopped tomatoes, stock, cod fillet, chickpeas and herbs.
4. Add the rest of the reserved chicken stock and simmer for 20-30 minutes.
5. Serve hot!

(Serves 2)

Calories per serving: 334, Protein: 28g, Carbs: 19g, Fat: 14g

ASIAN SPICED HALIBUT

Kick start your workout.

Ingredients

2X halibut fillets
A pinch of black pepper
2 Garlic cloves, pressed
2 Tbsp coconut oil
1 Lemon, juiced
1 Red chilli, diced
2 Green onions, sliced
1 Bok choy plant
1 Lime leaf
1 Tbsp fresh basil

How to make:

1. Preheat oven to 400°f/190°c/Gas Mark 5.
2. Add half of the ingredients into baking paper and fold into a parcel.
3. Add to the oven for 15-20 minutes or until fish thoroughly cooked through.
4. Serve this with your favorite vegetables, salad or even sweet potatoes.

(Serves 2)

Calories per serving: 354, Protein: 42g, Carbs: 2g, Fat: 18g

TERRIFIC TUNA NICOISE

King of the salads!

Ingredients

2X tuna steaks, each 1 inch thick
2 Tbsp olive oil,
2 Eggs
1 Tsp black pepper
1 Garlic clove, crushed
1 Tbsp capers
1/2 Cup green beans
1/2 Cup water
1 Lemon, juiced
1 Tsp fresh parsley, chopped
1/2 Iceberg lettuce (or similar)
1 Tsp balsamic vinegar
10 Cherry tomatoes
1/4 Red onion, thinly sliced

How to make:

1. Prepare the salad by washing and slicing the lettuce, tomatoes and onion and tossing together.
2. Mix 1 tbsp oil with the lemon juice, parsley and capers to form your salad dressing. Place to one side.
3. Boil a pan of water on a high heat then lower to simmer and add eggs for 6 minutes. Steam the green beans over the pan in a steamer/colander for the 6 minutes.
4. Meanwhile, brush the fish with 1 tbsp oil and then season with pepper.
5. Heat a skillet on a medium heat and sauté the garlic for 2-3 minutes.
6. Add the tuna steaks for about 2-3 minutes each side for medium-rare. (Add 1 minute each side for medium and 2 minutes each side for medium well).
7. Remove tuna from the skillet and allow to rest whilst you dress the salad with the dressing prepared earlier and toss through.

8. Rinse the eggs under cold water and peel before slicing in half.
9. Slice the tuna steaks and add to the salad with the eggs and green beans.

(Serves 2)

Calories per serving: 325, Protein: 42g, Carbs: 7g, Fat: 18g

SESAME MONKFISH & FRUIT SALSA

This fun tropical dish combines a great-tasting fish with a tangy salsa.

Ingredients

For the salsa:
1 Cup fresh mango, peeled and cubed
1/2 Red chili, finely chopped
1 Lime, juiced
2 Tsp cilantro, chopped
1 Onion, finely chopped
For the fish:
2 Monkfish fillets
2 Tsp olive oil
2 Tbsp sesame seeds

How to make:

1. Get a bowl and mix all of the ingredients for the salsa.
2. Drizzle 1 tbsp olive oil on the fillets and coat each side with the sesame seeds.
3. Heat 1 tbsp oil over a medium heat and then sauté the fillets for about 8 minutes each side or until the flesh flakes away.
4. Serve with the salsa on the side.

(Serves 2)

Calories per serving: 317, Protein: 18g, Carbs: 16g, Fat: 18g

GINGER & HONEY MAHI-MAHI WITH ORANGE SALAD

Aromatic and zingy! .

Ingredients

For the salad:
1 Orange, segmented
1/4 Red chili, finely chopped
1 Cup spinach leaves
1 Tsp balsamic vinegar
1 Tbsp olive oil
For the fish:
2X mahi mahi fillets
2 Tsp peanut oil
1 Tsp ginger, grated
1 Tbsp honey
1 Tbsp balsamic vinegar

How to make:

1. Get a bowl and mix all of the ingredients for the salad.
2. Mix the ginger, honey, oil and balsamic vinegar and then brush over the mahi-mahi.
3. Heat a skillet over a medium heat and then sauté the fillets for about 8 minutes each side or until the flesh flakes away.
4. Serve with the salad on the side. Season with salt and pepper to taste.

(Serves 2)

Calories per serving: 427, Protein: 30g, Carbs: 26g, Fat: 20g

SMOKED TROUT FISH CAKES

Great for lunch or dinner.

Ingredients

2 Large sweet potatoes, peeled and cubed
3 Tbsp extra virgin olive oil
1 Leek, chopped
4 Tsp dill, chopped
1 Tbsp grated orange peel
1 Pack smoked trout, sliced
1`/3 Cup low fat greek yogurt
(Optional)

How to make:

1. Preheat oven to 325°f/150°c/Gas Mark 3.
2. Lightly grease 2 ramekins or circular baking dishes with a little olive oil.
3. Heat the rest of the oil in a skillet over medium heat, and sauté the leeks and the potatoes for 5 minutes.
4. Lower the heat and cook for another 10 minutes until tender.
5. Transfer the potatoes and leeks to a separate bowl and crush with a fork to form a mash (alternatively use a potato masher).
6. Add the dill, orange peel and the trout and mix well.
7. Fill the ramekins with half the mixture each, patting to compact.
8. Bake for 15 minutes and remove.

Tip the ramekin out onto a plate, season and top with a dollop of Greek yogurt (optional).

(Serves 2)

Calories per serving: 529, Protein: 23g, Carbs: 47g, Fat: 26g

SCALLOPS WITH CAULIFLOWER & CHILI

We all deserve a treat now and then!

Ingredients

6 Queen or king scallops (row on)
1 Tbsp coconut oil
1/4 Cauliflower
1 Red chilli, diced
A pinch of black pepper
1 Lime, juiced

How to make:

1. Wash the cauliflower and remove any leaves. Use a sharp knife to cut very thin slices of cauliflower.
2. Add oil to a pan over a medium heat and add the cauliflower slices and chili for 3-4 minutes. Remove and place to one side.
3. Add the scallops to the same pan and squeeze over the lime juice.
4. Sauté for about 1 minute each side until lightly golden.
5. Plate up the cauliflower slices and place the scallops on top before seasoning with black pepper to taste.

(Serves 2)

Calories per serving: 164, Protein: 18g, Carbs: 6g, Fat: 8g

COCONUT SHRIMP & NOODLES

Crunchy shrimp with sweet & sour sauce.

Ingredients

8OZ Shrimp, Peeled And De Veined
1/4 Cup Coconut Flour
1/2 Tsp Cayenne Pepper
1 Tsp Garlic Powder
2 Beaten Free Range Eggs
1/2 Cup Shredded Coconut
1/4 Cup Almond Flour
A Pinch Of Black Pepper To Taste
1 Cup Cooked Noodles
1 Tsp Soy Sauce
1 Tsp Stevia
1/4 Cup Pineapple
1 Tsp Vinegar
1 Tbsp Ketchup

How to make:

1. Preheat oven to 400°f/200°c/Gas Mark 6.
2. Line a baking sheet with parchment paper.
3. Mix the coconut flour, cayenne pepper, and garlic powder in a bowl.
4. In a separate bowl, whisk the eggs.
5. In a third bowl, add the shredded coconut, almond flour and pepper.
6. Dip the shrimp into each dish in consecutive order, and then place on the baking sheet and bake for 10-15 minutes or until cooked through. Remove and place to one side.
7. Heat the soy sauce, ketchup, stevia, vinegar and pineapple with 1/2 cup water in a pan over a medium heat, stirring occasionally or until reduced.
8. Add to the cooked noodles in a pan until heated through and serve with the coconut shrimp on top.
9. Try with a side of broccoli.

(Serves 2)

Calories per serving: 455, Protein: 44g, Carbs: 52g, Fat: 15g

SPICY SWORDFISH STEAKS

If you can't get hold of swordfish, try this with tuna, shark or monk fish.

Ingredients

2X Swordfish Steaks, Skinless
2 Tbsp Onion Powder
2 Tsp Chili Powder
1 Garlic Clove, Minced
1/4 Cup Worcestershire Sauce
1 Tbsp Ground Black Pepper
2 Tbsp Thyme, Chopped

How to make:

1. In a bowl, mix all of the seasoning's and spices to form a paste before setting aside.
2. Spread a thin layer of paste on both sides of the fish, cover and chill for 30 minutes (If possible).
3. Preheat oven to 325°f/150°c/Gas Mark 3.
4. Bake the fish in parchment paper for 30-40 minutes, until well cooked.
5. Serve on a bed of quinoa or wholegrain couscous and your favorite salad.

(Serves 2)

Calories per serving: 455, Protein: 44g, Carbs: 52g, Fat: 15g

THAI TRAINING BROTH

Aromatic and spicy!

Ingredients

2X cod/haddock fillets
1 Tsp black pepper
1 Cup homemade chicken/veg broth
1 Cup water
1 Tsp coconut oil
1 Tsp five-spice powder
1 Tbsp olive oil
1 Cup pak choi
1/4 Cup sweetcorn
1 Tbsp ginger, minced
1 Cup noodles
1 Green onion, thinly sliced
2 Tsp cilantro, finely chopped

How to make:

1. In a bowl, combine pepper, 1/2 cup chicken broth, 1 cup water, coconut oil and spice blend.
2. Mix together and place to one side.
3. In a large saucepan, heat the oil on a medium heat and cook the pak choy and ginger for about 2 minutes until the bok choy is green.
4. Add the rest of the reserved chicken stock and heat through.
5. Add the noodles and stir, bringing to a simmer.
6. Add the green onion, sweetcorn and the fish and cook for 10-15 minutes until fish is tender.
7. Add the fish, noodles and vegetables into serving bowls and pour the broth over the top.
8. Garnish with the cilantro.

(Serves 2)

Calories per serving: 408, Protein: 35g, Carbs: 25g, Fat: 15g

GARLIC & LEMON SHRIMP LINGUINE

Amazing!

Ingredients

12 Oz shrimp, fresh or frozen
1 Garlic clove, minced
10 Cherry tomatoes, sliced in half
1 Tsp oregano
1 Cup whole wheat linguine
2 Tbsp olive oil
1/4 Cup green onions, chopped
1/2 Lemon, juiced

How to make:

1. If shrimp is frozen, allow to thoroughly defrost before cooking.
2. Heat a pan of water over a medium to high heat.
3. Once boiling, add linguine and lower heat to a simmer.
4. Cook according to package directions.
5. Meanwhile, heat 1 tbsp oil in a skillet over a medium heat.
6. Add the garlic, onions and tomatoes and sauté for 1-2 minutes.
7. Now add the prawns and cook thoroughly according to package directions.
8. Squeeze 1/4 lemon juice into the pan and shake gently for 1-2 minutes.
9. Drain the pasta and pour the shrimp, vegetables and all the lovely juices over the linguine and toss.
10. Drizzle the rest of the olive oil and lemon juice over the linguine to serve.

(Serves 2)

Calories per serving: 361, Protein: 47g, Carbs: 28g, Fat: 14g

MIGHTY MUSSEL BROTH

So easy to prepare!

Ingredients

10 Oz mussels (without their shells) or 2 cups mussels with shells
1 White onion. Finely diced
1 Lemon, juiced
1 Garlic clove, minced
1 Stalk celery, sliced
1/2 Cup veg stock
1/2 Cup canned tomatoes
2 Slices whole wheat bread
1 Tsp olive oil

How to make:

1. Heat the oil in a large pot over a medium heat.
2. Add the onion, garlic and celery and sauté for 4-5 minutes or until starting to soften.
3. Add the tomatoes, stock and lemon juice and bring to the boil.
4. Turn down the heat and allow to simmer for 10 minutes.
5. Add the mussels and cook according to package directions (this will depend on whether they are in their shell or out).
6. The flesh should be vibrant and orange once cooked and the shells will be open.
7. Lightly toast the bread and serve on the side.
8. Dunk in and enjoy!

(Serves 2)

Calories per serving: 447, Protein: 40g, Carbs: 39g, Fat: 14g

CHUNKY COD PARCELS

Succulent and juicy!

Ingredients

2X cod fillets, skinless & de-boned
10 Plum tomatoes
1 Lemon, halved
1/4 Cup olives, pitted
1 Tbsp olive oil
1 Garlic clove, halved
1/4 Red onion, sliced
1 Cup cooked whole-wheat couscous
1 Cup arugula

How to make:

1. Preheat oven to 400°f/200°c/Gas Mark 6.
2. Tear off two squares of parchment paper or foil.
3. Add a cod fillet, half the tomatoes, olives, onion, 1 garlic clove onto each sheet.
4. Squeeze the lemon juice over before popping in the wedge.
5. Place in the oven for 15-20 minutes or until cooked through.
6. Serve with couscous and a side of arugula with a drizzle of olive oil and a little black pepper.

(Serves 2)

Calories per serving: 394, Protein: 40g, Carbs: 49g, Fat: 11g

TUNA STEAKS WITH NUTTY GREEN

Meaty tuna steaks with crunchy greens!

Ingredients

2X 6oz tuna steaks, skinless
1 Cup green beans
1 Tbsp almonds, crushed
1 Garlic clove, minced
1 Tbsp olive oil
1 Tbsp black pepper corns, crushed
1 Tsp parsley

How to make:

1. Preheat the oven to its highest setting.
2. Layer the crushed almonds onto a baking tray and roast for 10-15 minutes.
3. Meanwhile, mix the oil with the garlic, pepper and parsley.
4. Marinate the tuna steaks for as long as possible.
5. Steam the green beans over a pot of boiling water for 4-6 minutes.
6. Heat a dry skillet on a medium to high heat.
7. Add the tuna steaks for about 2-3 minutes each side for medium-rare. (Add 1 minute each side for medium and 2 minutes each side for medium well).
8. Remove the tuna and allow to rest.
9. Scatter the roasted almonds over the green beans, season with a little black pepper and serve on the side of the tuna steak. Load up with sweet potato or quinoa if you're looking for extra calories or carbs.

(Serves 2)

Calories per serving: 447, Protein: 40g, Carbs: 39g, Fat: 14g

HADDOCK & KALE CRUMBLE

A lean fish pie!

Ingredients

4X haddock fillets, skinless & boneless
2 Cups curly kale
1/4 Cup whole-wheat breadcrumbs
1/2 Cup frozen peas
2 Cups rice milk/whole milk
1/4 Cup sesame seeds
1 Tsp black pepper
1 Tsp parsley

How to make:

1. Preheat oven to 400°f/200°c/Gas Mark 6.
2. Add the milk into a pan over a medium to high heat and bring to a simmer.
3. Add the haddock fillets, black pepper and parsley to the pan and lower the heat slightly.
4. Allow to simmer for 20-25 minutes or until cooked through.
5. Meanwhile, add the breadcrumbs and kale to a food processor and blitz together for 30 seconds (you still want a chunky texture).
6. Use a fork to flake the haddock fillets once cooked and return to the milk. Stir in the peas.
7. Into a deep oven dish, add the haddock and milk.
8. Top with the crispy kale mixture and bake in the oven for 25-30 minutes or until golden.

(Serves 2)

Calories per serving: 620, Protein: 66g, Carbs: 41g, Fat: 25g

SEAFOOD KEBABS & CUCUMBER SALAD

Get the BBQ ready!

Ingredients

6 King scallops
6 Whole shrimp
1 Cucumber
1 Tsp dill
1/2 Zucchini
2 Kebab sticks
1/2 Lime, juiced
1 Tbsp white wine vinegar

How to make:

1. Preheat the broiler or BBQ to a high heat.
2. Skewer the kebab sticks with the scallops and shrimp.
3. Squeeze the lemon juice over the top of the kebabs.
4. Broil on a lined baking tray for 4-5 minutes or until shrimp and scallops thoroughly cooked through.
5. Peel and slice the cucumber length ways.
6. Mix with the dill and white wine vinegar.
7. Serve the cucumber salad on the side of the kebabs.

(Serves 2)

Calories per serving: 121, Protein: 19g, Carbs: 8g, Fat: 1g

VEGETARIAN

While everyone knows that in order to build muscle, a diet rich in protein is necessary to supplement exercises and/or gym workouts, many people think that animal meat is the only rich source of protein. This is a myth. There are lots of veggies out there that are good, and even better, substitutes for meat.

The fact is, a vegetarian diet can also work for muscle building and in a much healthier way. For one, the risk of contracting heart disease, hypertension, diabetes, and other serious health conditions that are usually associated with consumption of meat products are definitely lessened.

This section will show you how you can whip up recipes that are not only healthy but are also easy to prepare; saving you a lot of precious time. In to-day's busy world, the ability to prepare quick and healthy meals will give you a decided advantage when working on your goals.

MUSCLE MUSHROOM WITH TOFU & QUINOA

A meaty mushroom flavor packed full of protein to keep your energy levels high and your motivation moving!

Ingredients

2 large Portabella mushrooms (dried and rinsed clean)
1/2 cup of cooked quinoa
1/2 cup of baby spinach
1/2 cup of kale
8oz of firm or extra firm tofu, press and crumble well
2 cherry tomatoes, sliced
½ onion, diced
1 tbsp of shredded non-fat mozzarella cheese
½ tbsp olive oil
¼ tbsp of paprika
1 crushed garlic clove, finely chopped
¼ tbsp of onion powder
¼ tbsp of cumin
Pinch of salt & pepper to taste

How to make:

1. Turn the grill on to high.
2. Get a large sauté pan and heat olive oil on a medium heat.
3. Toss in the tofu, kale and diced onion and sauté for around 3 minutes or until the onion starts to soften.
4. Add the spices, salt & pepper, and quinoa. Sauté for a couple of minutes more.
5. Place the portabello mushrooms on a baking sheet and lightly brush with olive oil. Stack the mushroom cap with quinoa mixture, spinach, shredded cheese, and sliced tomatoes.
6. Grill for another 5 minutes, and then serve immediately. Enjoy!

(Serves 2)

Calories per serving: 366, Protein: 20g, Carbs: 40g, Fat: 14g

TASTY TEMPEH RICE BOWL

This protein-packed recipe is great for lunch or dinner on a regular day. Use the leftover veggies in the fridge and give them an exciting twist with some creativity

Ingredients

4oz of tempeh (crumbled)
1 cup of cooked brown rice
8 cherry tomatoes, diced
½ red bell pepper, sliced
½ green bell pepper, sliced
1 tbsp of soy sauce
½ tsp of ginger
½ tsp of onion powder
1 garlic clove, finely diced & crushed
½ tsp of chilli paste
1 sliced green onion

How to make:

1. Put some olive oil in a large-sized sauté pan and heat over medium setting.
2. Toss in the bell peppers, tomatoes and onion and stir until softened lightly.
3. Add the rest of the ingredients to the pan apart from the tempeh and the rice.
4. Get another pan and pre-heat over medium setting. Add the tempeh.
5. Allow to cook for around 5 minutes. Stir from time to time.
6. Put brown rice in a bowl and top with tempeh, green onions, and other veggies. Serve hot and enjoy!

(Serves 1)

Calories per serving: 246, Protein: 23g, Carbs: 94g, Fat: 13g

SPEEDY BLACK BEAN SURPRISE

If you're craving the distinct taste of an authentic Mexican meal, this recipe can solve your problem – without the usual grease that comes hand in hand with the takeaway version!.

Ingredients

1/2 cup of freshly cooked brown rice
1/2 cup of freshly cooked quinoa
1/2 cup of freshly cooked bulghar wheat
Handful of black olives
3oz of cooked black beans
¼ avocado, sliced
2 tbsp of plain non-fat Greek yogurt
2 tbsp of salsa
A generous dash of hot sauce

How to make:

1. Get a big bowl and mix all the ingredients together.
2. Enjoy your authentic Mexican meal.

(Serves 2)

Calories per serving: 550, Protein: 25g, Carbs: 90g, Fat: 10g

BRAWNY VEG LASAGNA

Very low in fat and vegan, this is a quick and easy to prepare crockpot meal using only a few ingredients and very filling too

Ingredients

½ pack of soft tofu
½ pack of firm tofu
4oz of whole wheat lasagne sheets (1/2 box)
1 cup of baby spinach
4 tbsp of almond milk
¼ tsp of garlic powder
Juice of ½ a lemon
1 ½ tbsp of fresh basil, chopped
1 can of chopped tomatoes
Black pepper to taste
1 diced courgette/zucchini
½ tsp of salt

How to make:

1. Preheat oven to (325°F/170 °C/Gas Mark 3).
2. Process the soft and firm tofu, garlic powder, almond milk, basil, lemon juice and salt in a blender until smooth. Toss in the spinach and courgette.
3. Put about 1/3 of chopped tomatoes at the bottom of an oven dish.
4. Top the sauce with 1/3 of the lasagne sheets and 1/3 of the spinach/tofu mixture. Repeat the layers finishing with the chopped tomatoes on top.
5. Cook for around 1 hour or until the pasta sheets are soft.

(Serves 2)

Calories per serving: 355, Protein: 20g, Carbs: 50g, Fat: 15g

BRAWNY BLACK BEAN & COTTAGE CHEESE FAJITA

A taste of the classic Mexican dish, but with a vegetarian twist, this dish is just as appetizing but a lot healthier.

Ingredients

5oz of cooked and washed black beans
3.5oz of cannellini beans, cooked
4oz of red kidney beans, cooked
1 green pepper, sliced
1 yellow pepper, sliced
1 onion, sliced
1 beef tomato, chopped
3oz of cottage cheese
1 packet of fajita seasoning
4 whole wheat flour tortillas
2 tbsp salsa
2 tbsp of olive oil

How to make:

1. Preheat the oven to (250°F/130 °C/Gas Mark 1/2).
2. In a pan on a medium heat, sauté the onions and peppers for around 2 to 4 minutes. Stir often and make sure not to overcook.
3. Add to the black beans and transfer to a oven proof dish.
4. Keep the dish warm by placing it in the oven as you prepare the other ingredients.
5. Dice the tomato and set aside.
6. Microwave the tortillas to slightly heat them up.
7. Assemble the fajitas.
8. Serve and enjoy!

(Serves 2)

Calories per serving: 412, Protein: 25g, Carbs: 60g, Fat: 8g

VEGGIE BRAWN BURGER

You're not

Ingredients

4oz of extra firm tempah
1 tsp of red chilli flakes
½ tbsp of Sriracha (hot chilli sauce)
1 diced red pepper
¼ piece of small sized red onion
Handful of baby spinach
½ tbsp of teriyaki marinade
1 whole wheat bun

How to make:

1. Heat the grill, and then marinate the tempah in Sriracha, red chilli flakes and teriyaki marinade.
2. Sauté the onion in a pan on a medium heat until it is caramelized. Stir in the pepper and baby spinach for a further 3-4 minutes.
3. Grill the tempah for around 4 minutes on each side.
4. Lay down the tempah in the bun and then add the caramelized onion, spinach and diced peppers.
5. Serve immediately while hot. Enjoy!

(Serves 1)

Calories per serving: 162, Protein: 26g, Carbs: 40g, Fat: 13g

TOFU LETTUCE WRAPS

Tasty and easy to prepare, this is will make a great on-the-go lunch.

Ingredients

½ pack of tofu, crumbled
1 head baby gem lettuce or equivalent
½ small onion, chopped
½ red bell pepper, chopped
½ tbsp of garlic, chopped
½ tbsp of olive oil
½ tbsp of soy sauce
½ tsp of ginger powder
½ tsp of onion powder
½ tsp of garlic powder

How to make:

1. Get a large pan and heat olive oil over a medium heat setting.
2. Sauté tofu, onion, and bell pepper for about 3-4 minutes.
3. Put the soy sauce and other spices into the pan and allow sauté for 2 minutes more.
4. Add the tofu mix to the lettuce leaves.
5. Serve while hot

(Serves 2)

Calories per serving: 190, Protein: 18g, Carbs: 12g, Fat: 10g

BLACK BEAN VEGGIE BURGERS

Tasty and easy to make – two qualities that every busy vegetarian bodybuilder loves. These veggie burgers are wholesome and satisfying

Ingredients

½ onion, chopped
5oz of black beans, well drained
1/4 cup of flour
1 slice of bread, crumbled into bread crumbs
½ tsp of seasoned salt
1 tsp of onion powder
1 tsp of garlic powder
Pinch of salt & pepper to taste
1 tsp of olive oil

How to make:

1. In a pan over a medium heat, sautee the onions for 3 to 5 minutes or until soft.
2. Mash the beans in a large bowl until almost smooth, then add the sautéed onion, salt, bread-crumbs, onion powder, and garlic powder. Mix well to combine.
3. Add flour, 1 or 2 tbsp at a time. The mixture will thicken.
4. Shape into patties, about ½" thick.
5. Fry patties in a little oil at medium-low heat setting until lightly browned and firm on each side.
6. Make the burgers and serve.

(Serves 2)

Calories per serving: 337, Protein: 18g, Carbs: 55g, Fat: 11g

SPICY SEITAN STRIPS

Seitan is a chewy, protein-rich vegetarian option and adds a chunky texture and moreish flavour to this dish.

Ingredients

12oz of seitan, sliced
1 tsp of onion powder
1 tbsp of cayenne pepper
2 tsp of garlic powder
dash of hot sauce
50g of baby spinach
2 tbsp of olive oil

How to make:

1. Coat the seitan with onion powder and garlic powder.
2. Fry in olive oil for 5 to 7 minutes at medium-high heat setting.
3. Get a medium bowl, and mix the hot sauce with the seitan in the bowl.
4. Coat well by stirring.
5. Serve on a bed of baby spinach.

(Serves 4)

Calories per serving: 138, Protein: 20g, Carbs: 10g, Fat: 2g

FETA & BRAWNY BARLEY STUFFED PORTABELLAS

This is a unique and healthy entree recipe for vegetarians in need of a high-fiber, high-protein meal.

Ingredients

4 large portabella mushrooms
1/2 cup of cooked quinoa
4oz of feta cheese, crumbled
1 red bell pepper, chopped
1 chopped beef tomato
1/3 cup of water
½ cucumber, chopped
1 green onion, sliced
4 tsp of olive oil
1 tbsp of Dijon mustard
1 tbsp of white wine vinegar
Pinch of salt and pepper

How to make:

1. Preheat the grill.
2. Combine the cooked quinoa, bell pepper, feta, cucumber, green onion, mustard, white wine vinegar in a medium-sized bowl.
3. Place the portabella mushrooms on a baking sheet and lightly brush with olive oil. Stack the mushroom caps with the quinoa mixture.
4. Place under the grill for 5 minutes, then serve immediately. Enjoy!

(Serves 2)

Calories per serving: 322, Protein: 25g, Carbs: 33g, Fat: 10g

RUSTIC GARLIC PROTEIN QUINOA

While this is a basic and simple recipe, it is flexible and can be modified to include other veggies or leftovers; you can also add tofu for more protein..

Ingredients

1oz of mozzarella cheese
2oz of cooked kidney beans
1 cup of uncooked quinoa
1 cupof vegetable broth
1 onion, diced
4 cloves of garlic, minced
1/4 tsp of salt
1 tbsp olive oil

How to make:

1. Sautee garlic and onion in olive oil in a pan at medium heat until onions soften. Lower heat.
2. Add the quinoa and vegetable broth. Cover the pan and simmer for around 15 to 20 minutes or until quinoa is soft and liquid is significantly absorbed.
3. Top with cheese and beans and serve with salt to taste.

(Serves 3)

Calories per serving: 292, Protein: 15g, Carbs: 40g, Fat: 8g

JASON'S SUN DRIED TOMATO & WALNUT PENNE PASTA

If you love sun-dried tomatoes, then you will definitely enjoy this gourmet pasta dish.

Ingredients

1.5 cup of whole-wheat pasta
2 cloves of garlic, minced
2oz of walnuts, coarsely chopped
1/4 cup of sun-dried tomatoes, drained & chopped, in oil
2 tbsp of olive oil
1 tsp of basil
4oz of low-fat mozzarella cheese
Pinch of salt

How to make:

1. Boil a large saucepan of water.
2. Add the pasta and cook following directions on the package.
3. While the pasta is cooking, prepare the sauce. Put minced garlic in a bowl.
4. Add sun-dried tomatoes, walnuts, basil, mozzarella and oil.
5. Once the pasta is cooked, drain it and add to the sauce.
6. Toss through until the pasta is well coated.
7. Transfer the dish onto a serving plate.
8. Serve.

(Serves 4)

Calories per serving: 375, Protein: 20g, Carbs: 40g, Fat: 15g

VEGETARIAN DELI SANDWICH

This is a healthy on-the-go lunch for vegetarian bodybuilders. Packed with protein and fibre, this recipe is simple and easy to prepare..

Ingredients

4 tbsp of hummus
2 tbsp of chia seeds
Handful of baby spinach
1/4 of avocado, sliced thinly
1 slice of beef tomato
2 slices of Ezekiel bread

How to make:

1. Get one slice of bread and put hummus on 1 side.
2. Put the lettuce and avocado and tomato on the top.
3. Top with the other bread slice.
4. Serve and enjoy.

(Serves 1)

Calories per serving: 570, Protein: 26g, Carbs: 70g, Fat: 22g

CHEESE, FRUIT AND SPINACH MELTS

Low in calories yet loaded with protein, you cannot go wrong with this easy to prepare lunch sandwich.

Ingredients

4 slices of Ezekiel bread
1 piece of apple, thinly sliced
4oz of grated low fat cheese
2 tsp of mustard
1/2 cup of spinach

How to make:

1. Pre-heat Panini/sandwich press (or non-stick skillet) over a medium heat setting.
2. Spread mustard lightly and evenly on each bread slice.
3. Layer the slices of apples, spinach and cheese on 2 bread slices. Top with the remaining 2 slices of bread.
4. Coat the Panini press (or skillet) with cooking spray, and grill the sandwiches for around 5 minutes or until the bread is toasted and cheese is melted.
5. Remove from the pan and set aside to cool slightly.
6. Serve.

(Serves 2)

Calories per serving: 395, Protein: 22g, Carbs: 43g, Fat: 15g

SUPER SPAGHETTI SQUASH

A healthy variation to the popular Italian favourite, loaded with protein for muscle building.

Ingredients

16oz of tempeh , cubed
1 spaghetti squash or pumpkin, halved and deseeded
3 tbsp of tamari or soy sauce
2 tbsp of mirin
1 can of chopped tomatoes
1 tbsp of olive oil
2 cloves of garlic, chopped finely
1/2 cup of small broccoli florets
1/2 cup of baby spinach

How to make:

1. Pre-heat the oven to (375°F/190 °C/Gas Mark 5).
2. Get a medium-sized bowl and toss together the tamari, tempeh, garlic, and mirin. Marinate and set aside for 30 minutes.
3. Get a large baking dish and arrange the squash halves with the cut sides down. Pour half a cup of water into the dish. Bake for around 45 minutes or until tender. Take the dish out of the oven. Turn the squash over and allow to slightly cool.
4. Get a large skillet and heat oil at medium heat. Add tempeh and cook for 7 to 8 minutes until golden brown, occasionally stirring. Remove the tempeh and keep warm on a plate.
5. In a medium-sized pot, heat chopped tomatoes at medium heat, and then add the broccoli and allow to cook until tender (around 5 minutes.) Stir the spinach in and remove from heat.
6. Use a fork to scrape off spaghetti squash strands onto a platter. Spoon some broccoli and hot chopped tomatoes over the dish. Serve with tempeh on top.

(Serves 4)

Calories per serving: 295, Protein: 20g, Carbs: 20g, Fat: 15g

JASON'S QUINOA & CHICKPEA INFUSION

This is another comfort dish which tastes great!

Ingredients

1 can of chickpeas
Handful of diced olives
1 cup quinoa, rinsed
1 cup of chopped tomatoes
1/4 cup of vegetable broth
2 pieces of squash, diced
2 cloves of garlic, chopped
½ onion, diced
1 red onion, diced
1 tsp of oregano
1 tsp of basil
1 tsp of thyme

How to make:

1. Sauté the onion, garlic, and squash in a large-sized saucepan over a medium heat.
2. Put the tomatoes in to the pan and allow to cook for 5 minutes.
3. Pour in the broth and boil.
4. Next, add the quinoa and chickpeas. Cover and lower the heat. Allow to cook for about 10 to 15 minutes or until most of the water is absorbed.
5. Add the herbs and olives and stir through.
6. Remove from saucepan and serve.

(Serves 3)

Calories per serving: 305, Protein: 15g, Carbs: 50g, Fat: 5g

MUSCLE MILLET & QUINOA

A light dish just right for a relaxing rest day or a day off from your muscle building work-outs.

Ingredients

1 cup of millet
1 cup of quinoa
1 diced banana
½ litre of almond milk
½ litre of water
½ tsp of ground ginger
½ cinnamon stick
2 pieces of star anise
2 pieces of cardamom pods
1 tsp of honey

How to make:

1. Use a sieve to rinse the millet and quinoa under cold running water.
2. Tip into the crockpot.
3. Boil water in a pan over a high heat and add the spices and almond milk. Pour everything into the crockpot.
4. Put the lid on and set heat to low. Cook for 8 to 9 hours or overnight.
5. The porridge dish should be creamy and rich when done.
6. Ladle into bowls and pour over some honey for a treat.
7. Serve with diced banana.

(Serves 2)

Calories per serving: 409, Protein: 11g, Carbs: 80g, Fat: 5g

TITAN CHILI TOFU

This is a great tasting tofu dish that is easy to prepare; ideal for when you like to spice things up a bit!.

Ingredients

4oz of extra-firm tofu, drained, divided into 4 pieces
1 tbsp of rice vinegar
1 tbsp of soy sauce
½ tsp of hot chili sauce
½ tsp of ginger, minced
A pinch of salt and black pepper

How to make:

1. Combine vinegar, soy sauce, chilli sauce, and ginger in a small bowl.
2. Sprinkle the tofu with salt & pepper.
3. Heat a non-stick skillet over a medium heat. Cook the tofu until browned on both sides, or 3 minutes for each side.
4. Add the soy sauce mixture and cook for half a minute, constantly stirring.
5. Transfer to serving dish.

(Serves 1)

Calories per serving: 329, Protein: 30g, Carbs: 10g, Fat: 19g

BRAWNY TOFU STEAKS

For the new vegetarian bodybuilder who is new to tofu dishes, this is one good way to introduce this vegetarian ingredient.

Ingredients

10oz of extra firm tofu
2 tsp of garlic powder
2 tsp of coriander, ground
2 tsp of chilli powder
½ cup of tamari

How to make:

1. Cut the tofu into slices.
2. Combine all other ingredients in one bowl. Pour the mixture over the slices.
3. Allow to marinate for an hour, store in the refrigerator in a sealed container.
4. Fry in a little olive oil over a medium heat for 7-8 minutes.
5. Serve with cooked rice or noodles..

(Serves 2)

Calories per serving: 315, Protein: 30g, Carbs: 15g, Fat: 15g

BRAWNY BARLEY & QUINOA CASSEROLE

Barley is high in fibre and protein and this is a great warm dish to fuel you through your workouts.

Ingredients

1 cup of barley
1 cup of cooked quinoa
1 green chilli, finely chopped
3 cups of water
8oz cheddar cheese, shredded
1/4 cup of sour cream

How to make:

1. Get a lidded saucepan and boil water over a high heat.
2. Add the barley, and continue to boil. Set heat to low. Cook with lid on for around 45 minutes or until the liquid is significantly absorbed and the barley is tender. Take off the heat and allow to cool slightly.
3. Mix barley with the shredded cheese, quinoa, chillies, and sour cream in a large-sized bowl.
4. Serve and enjoy.

(Serves 6)

Calories per serving: 315, Protein: 30g, Carbs: 15g, Fat: 15g

TRAINING TOFU BROTH

Tofu is a protein source and soaks up all the flavors it's cooked in.

Ingredients

1 Pack of drained, pressed and cubed tofu
1 Tbsp coconut oil
1/2 Onion, sliced
1 Cup udon noodles/brown rice,
1 Cup of sugar snap peas
1/2 Chili, finely sliced
1/2 Cup coconut milk
1/2 Cup (homemade) veg stock
1 Bok choy
1 Tbsp lime juice
1/2 Cup water chestnuts
1/4 Cup green onions, sliced

How to make:

1. Heat the oil in a wok on a high heat and then sauté the tofu until brown on each side.
2. Add the onion and sauté for 2-3 minutes.
3. Add the coconut milk and stock to the wok until it starts to bubble.
4. Lower to a medium heat and add the noodles, chili and water chestnuts.
5. Allow to simmer for 10-15 minutes and then add the bok choy and sugar snap peas for 5 minutes.
6. Serve with a sprinkle of green onions.

(Serves 2)

Calories per serving: 517, Protein: 24g, Carbs: 67g, Fat: 31g

MEXICAN BEANS & QUINOA

Beans are a great source of vitamins and fibre as well as protein. These taste amazing..

Ingredients

1 Tbsp olive oil
1 Cup of quinoa
1 Onion, diced
1 Garlic clove, diced
1 Tsp oregano
1 Tsp parsley
1/2 Cup black beans
1/2 Cup kidney beans
1/4 Cup red lentils, soaked
1 Avocado, sliced
2 Tbsp of plain non-fat greek
Yogurt
1 Tsp paprika
1 Tsp chili flakes
1 Tbsp fresh cilantro
1 Lemon, juiced

How to make:

1. Heat a pan of water on a high heat and add quinoa, allowing to cook for 15 minutes.
2. In a separate pan heat the oil over a medium heat and add the onions and garlic to sauté for 3-4 minutes.
3. Now add the beans and lentils as well as the oregano and parsley and stir through.
4. Add 1 cup of water and allow the beans to simmer for 20-25 minutes or until soft.
5. Meanwhile, in a separate bowl, crush the avocado into the yogurt with a fork and squeeze in a little lemon juice. Sprinkle with paprika.
6. Once quinoa has soaked up most of the liquid, add the rest of the lemon juice and a little salt

and pepper.

7. Serve with the beans (the liquid should have been absorbed and the beans and lentils soft) and the avocado dip.
8. Enjoy!

(Serves 4)

Calories per serving: 329, Protein: 12g, Carbs: 50g, Fat: 13g

VEGAN LASAGNE

Creamy, bubbling lasagne!.

Ingredients

1/2 Pack of soft tofu
1 Cup of almond milk
1 Red onion, diced
1 Garlic clove, minced
1 Tsp oregano
1 Tsp basil
1 Can of chopped tomatoes
A pinch of black pepper to taste
1 Zucchini , sliced
1 Red pepper, sliced
1 Eggplant, sliced
1 Tbsp olive oil

How to make:

1. Preheat oven to 325°F/170 °C/Gas Mark 3.
2. Slice zucchini, eggplant and pepper into vertical strips (think lasagne sheets).
3. Add the almond milk and tofu to a food processor and blitz until smooth. Place to one side.
4. Heat the oil in a skillet over a medium heat and add the onions and garlic for 3-4 minutes or until soft.
5. Now add the canned tomatoes, herbs and pepper and allow to stir through for 5-6 minutes until hot.
6. Into a lasagne or suitable oven dish, layer 1/3

the eggplant, followed by 1/3 zucchini, then 1/3 pepper before pouring over 1/3 of the tomato sauce and 1/3 tofu white sauce.

7. Repeat for the next 2 layers, finishing with the white sauce.
8. Add to the oven for 40-50 minutes or until veg is soft and can easily by sliced into servings.

(Serves 2)

Calories per serving: 301, Protein: 18g, Carbs: 15g, Fat: 15g

TOASTED SESAME & PEANUT TOFU

Aromatic & energizing!

Ingredients

1 Pack firm tofu, pressed & cubed
1/4 Cup sesame seeds
1 Tbsp smooth whole peanut butter
1 Tbsp almond or rice milk
1 Cup tenderstem broccoli/green beans
1/2 Lime, juiced
1 Tbsp coconut oil

How to make:

1. Add the peanut butter to the milk and whisk until loosened and add to a shallow bowl.
2. Add sesame seeds to a shallow bowl.
3. Once the tofu has been pressed for as long as possible (to get rid of extra liquid), dip each cube into the peanut milk to cover and then dip straight into the sesame seeds to coat. If they don't cover perfectly don't worry!
4. Heat the oil in a wok or skillet over a high heat.
5. Once hot, add the tofu to the pan and pour in any extra peanut milk and seeds.
6. Allow to cook for 10-15 minutes, occasionally turning to brown each side.
7. Meanwhile, boil a pan of water and add the broccoli/green beans and cook to package

guidelines.

8. Serve the tofu on a bed of greens and enjoy.

(Serves 2)

Calories per serving: 370, Protein: 21g, Carbs: 9g, Fat: 25g

HALLOUMI BURGERS & CHILI KETCHUP

Possibly better than a beef burger!

Ingredients

4 Slices halloumi cheese
2 Wholegrain pitta breads
1/4 Cup arugula
1/2 Cup button mushrooms, diced
1 Red chili, finely diced
1 Cup tomatoes
1 Tsp stevia
1 Tbsp olive oil
1 Red onion, diced

How to make:

1. Prepare the chili ketchup by heating the oil in a skillet over a medium heat. Add the onions and sweat for 3-4 minutes.
2. Now add the fresh tomatoes, mushrooms and chili and turn down the heat.
3. Leave to simmer whilst preparing the burgers - add a tbsp water to stop it sticking.
4. Meanwhile, heat a griddle pan or broiler on a medium to high heat and add the halloumi slices for 5-10 minutes.
5. Lightly toast the pitta breads.
6. Place the tomato mixture (which should be nice and thick by now) into a food processor and blend until smooth. If you don't have one don't worry - the ketchup is still great chunky
7. Serve the halloumi in the pitta with the arugula and chili ketchup.

(Serves 2)

Calories per serving: 417, Protein: 19g, Carbs: 22g, Fat: 19g

STRONG SPAGHETTI SQUASH QUINOA

A hearty dish to build strength.

Ingredients

1 Spaghetti squash, halved and deseeded
1 Tbsp of extra virgin olive oil
1/2 Cup quinoa
1 Tsp rosemary, chopped
1 Tsp tarragon
1 Tsp black pepper

How to make:

1. Pre-heat the oven to 375°F/190 °C/Gas Mark 5.
2. Grab a large baking dish and arrange the squash halves with the cut side down and pour half a cup of water into the dish.
3. Bake for around 45 minutes or until tender and remove the dish from the oven. Turn the squash over and allow to slightly cool.
4. Meanwhile, heat a pan of water on a medium to high heat and add oil and quinoa as well as the herbs. Bring to a boil and then turn down the heat and allow to simmer for 15 minutes.
5. Once the quinoa has soaked up most of the liquid, place the lid on the pan and allow to steam.
6. Use a fork to scrape the flesh from the spaghetti squash and then dice.
7. Stir through the quinoa and add a little black pepper and extra oil to serve if desired.

(Serves 2)

Calories per serving: 400, Protein: 12g, Carbs: 63g, Fat: 11g

SPICED CAULIFLOWER & CHICKPEA CURRY

This dish is full of flavor and texture and the protein from the chickpeas adds up!

Ingredients

1 Cauliflower, florets
2 Cup chickpeas (canned or soaked)
1 Onion, diced
1 Garlic clove, minced
1 Tsp cumin
1 Tsp turmeric
1 Tsp garam masala
1/2 Chili, diced
1 Tbsp coconut oil
1 Tbsp fresh cilantro, chopped to garnish
1/2 Cup chopped tomatoes
1/2 Cup water
1/4 Cup greek yogurt (optional)

How to make:

1. In a skillet, add the oil and heat on a medium heat.
2. Add the onion and garlic and stir for 5 minutes until soft.
3. Add the cumin, turmeric and garam masala and stir to release the aromas.
4. Now add the chili to the pan along with the chickpeas and cauliflower. Stir to coat in the spices.
5. Pour in the tomatoes and water and reduce the heat to simmer for 30 minutes or until chickpeas soft.
6. Garnish with cilantro to serve as well as a dollop of yogurt if desired.

(Serves 2)

Calories per serving: 410, Protein: 19g, Carbs: 59g, Fat: 11g

GARLIC STUFFED MUSHROOMS

Portabella mushrooms are a meal in themselves!

Ingredients

4 Large portabella mushrooms
1/2 Cup of quinoa, cooked
2 Garlic cloves, minced
1 Beef tomato, sliced
1 Tbsp of extra virgin olive oil
1 Tbsp thyme
Pinch of black pepper

How to make:

1. Preheat the broiler to a medium high heat.
2. Remove the stems from the mushrooms and place to one side.
3. Combine the cooked quinoa, garlic, tomato, oil, black pepper, mushroom stems and thyme and add to a food processor to blitz.
4. Place the portabella mushrooms on a baking sheet and lightly brush with olive oil.
5. Stack the mushroom caps with the quinoa mixture.
6. Place under the broiler for 10 minutes, then serve hot.

(Serves 2)

Calories per serving: 406, Protein: 15g, Carbs: 63g, Fat: 11g

CREAMY WALNUT PENNE

A low fat creamy sauce goes brilliantly with the nutty textures.

Ingredients

1 Cup 100% wholegrain pasta
1 Cup almond milk
1/2 Cup cottage cheese
1/4 Cup of walnuts, coarsely chopped
1 Tbsp tarragon
Pinch of black pepper
1/2 Cup spinach leaves

How to make:

1. Boil a large saucepan of water on a high heat.
2. Add the pasta and cook following directions on the package.
3. While the pasta is cooking, prepare the sauce:
4. Whisk the cottage cheese with the almond milk until the lumps have gone (alternatively use a food processor).
5. Once the pasta is cooked, drain and add the white sauce over a low heat.
6. Toss through until the pasta is well coated and the sauce is hot.
7. Add the walnuts, spinach and tarragon and stir well until the spinach has wilted.
8. Transfer onto a serving plate and sprinkle with a little black pepper.

(Serves 2)

Calories per serving: 291, Protein: 16g, Carbs: 28g, Fat: 13g

PUMPKIN & PINE NUT CASSEROLE

Hearty stew with a crunchy topping.

Ingredients

2 Tbsp extra virgin olive oil
1 Cup red onion, chopped
1 Pumpkin
1 Tsp black pepper
1 Tsp chili powder
1 Bay leaf
3 Tbsp pine nuts
1 Tbsp paprika
1 Tbsp thyme
1 Tsp black pepper
1 Cup veg stock
1/2 Cup chopped tomatoes
2 Cup cooked quinoa

How to make:

1. Prepare the pumpkin by using a sharp knife to remove the 'lid' and then scooping out the flesh with a spoon/fork.
2. Heat the oil in a pot over a medium to high heat and add the red onion for 5 minutes.
3. Season with herbs and spices before adding in pumpkin flesh and stirring for 5 minutes.
4. Add tomatoes, bay leaf and stock, cover and simmer for 40-45 minutes or until pumpkin soft.
5. Meanwhile preheat the oven to its highest temperature.
6. Serve with your choice of brown rice or quinoa and scatter the pine nuts over the top.

(Serves 4)

Calories per serving: 438, Protein: 13g, Carbs: 64g, Fat: 14g

CHINESE TEMPAH STIR FRY

Tempah is a great source of protein.

Ingredients

1 Tbsp coconut oil
1 Clove garlic, minced
1 Thumb sized piece fresh ginger, minced
1 Pack tempah, sliced
1/2 Cup green onions
1/2 Cup bean sprouts
1/2 Cup baby corn/sweetcorn
1 Cup brown rice, cooked

How to make:

1. Heat the oil in a skillet or wok on a high heat and add the garlic, spices and ginger.
2. Cook for 1 minute.
3. Now add the tempah and cook for 5-6 minutes before adding the bean sprouts and baby corn for a further 10 minutes.
4. Now add the green onions and serve over brown rice.

(Serves 2)

Calories per serving: 392, Protein: 19g, Carbs: 42g, Fat: 20g

AESTHETIC ASPARAGUS & BEETROOT TART

Pastry-free tart with the crisp freshness of the asparagus with the sweet edge of the beetroot.

Ingredients

1 Tbsp coconut oil
1/2 Cup asparagus
1/2 Cup cooked beetroot
6 Eggs
1 Cup coconut milk
1 Tsp black pepper

How to make:

1. Preheat the broiler to a medium heat.
2. Whisk the eggs and coconut milk in a separate bowl.
3. On a medium heat, heat the coconut oil in an oven proof (steel) frying pan, adding in the asparagus and beetroot and sautéing for 5 minutes.
4. Add the egg mix to the pan with the vegetables in and continue to cook on the stove (low heat) for 7 minutes until it becomes light and bubbly.
5. Finish the tart in its pan under the broiler for a further 5 -10 minutes or until crispy on the top and cooked through.
6. Slice and serve hot or allow to cool and serve chilled from the fridge

(Serves 4)

Calories per serving: 156, Protein: 10g, Carbs: 3g, Fat: 11G

RAISIN & ROOT VEG STEW

A vegetarian take on this classic dish.

Ingredients

2 Tbsp olive oil
1 Onion, diced
2 Turnips, peeled and diced
2 Cloves of garlic
1 Tsp ground cumin
1/2 Tsp ground ginger
1/2 Tsp ground cinnamon
1/4 Tsp cayenne pepper
1/2 Cup carrots, peeled and diced
2 Parsnips, peeled and diced
1 Sweet potato, peeled and diced
2 Cups homemade vegetable stock
1/4 Cup fresh parsley, chopped
1/4 Cup raisins
1 Cup cooked quinoa

How to make:

1. In a large pot, heat the oil on a medium high heat before sautéing the onion for 4-5 minutes until soft.
2. Add the turnip, sweet potato and parsnip and cook for 10 minutes or until golden brown.
3. Add the garlic, cumin, ginger, cinnamon, and cayenne pepper, cooking for a further 3 minutes.
4. Add the carrots, raisins and stock to the pot and then bring to the boil.
5. Turn the heat down to a medium heat, cover and simmer for 20 minutes.
6. Garnish with the parsley and serve with the quinoa

(Serves 2)

Calories per serving: 642, Protein: 15g, Carbs: 105g, Fat: 15G

SPANISH PAELLA

A delicious protein packed meal!.

Ingredients

1 Tbsp extra virgin olive oil
1/2 Red bell pepper, chopped
1/2 Yellow bell pepper, chopped
1/2 Zucchini, chopped
1/2 Red onion, chopped
1 Cup brown rice
1 Lemon
1 Tsp paprika
1 Tsp oregano (dried)
1 Tsp parsley (dried)
1 Cup homemade vegetable stock
1 Cup red lentils, soaked

How to make:

1. Add rice and lentils to a pot of cold water and cook for 15 minutes.
2. Drain the water, cover the pan and leave to one side.
3. Heat the oil in a skillet and add the bell pepper,s onion and zucchini, sautéing for 5 minutes.
4. To the pan, add the rice, lentils, herb, spices and juice of the lemon along with the vegetable stock/water.
5. Cover and turn heat right down and allow to simmer for 15-20 minutes.
6. Serve hot.

(Serves 2)

Calories per serving: 345, Protein: 12g, Carbs: 50g, Fat: 9G

KINO KEDGEREE

A vegetarian take on this classic dish.

Ingredients

2 Onions, cut into quarters
1/2 Cup broccoli
1/4 Cauliflower
1 Tbsp extra virgin olive oil
1 Tbsp curry powder
1 Cup brown rice, rinsed thoroughly
2 Eggs
1 Tsp black pepper
1 Tbsp fresh chives, chopped

How to make:

1. Preheat the oven to 375°f/190°c/Gas Mark 5.
2. Add the vegetables to an oven dish and toss together.
3. Drizzle with oil and sprinkle with curry powder and pepper - toss to coat.
4. Bake in the oven for 30 minutes, stirring occasionally.
5. Meanwhile add the rice to a pot of cold water and bring to the boil over a high heat.
6. Simmer for 15 minutes until rice has nearly soaked up all of the water.
7. Turn the heat to the lowest temperature and cover the pan for a further 5 minutes until light and fluffy.
8. Boil a separate pan of water and add the eggs for 7 minutes.
9. Run under the cold tap, crack and peel the eggs before cutting in half.
10. Toss the rice with the roasted vegetables and top with eggs and chopped chives.
11. Serve hot!

(Serves 2)

Calories per serving: 287, Protein: 10g, Carbs: 33g, Fat: 12G

ZESTY ZUCCHINI PASTA & PROTEIN PEAS

Gloriously healthy homemade pasta with a crunchy topping. .

Ingredients

1 Cup frozen peas
1 Tbsp fresh mint, chopped
1/2 Cup greek yogurt
4 Zucchinis, peeled and sliced
Vertically to make noodles (use a spiralizer)
1 Tsp black pepper
1 Tsp honey
1 Tsp red chili flakes
1 Tbsp extra virgin olive oil
1/2 Cup arugula
1/2 Lemon, juiced

How to make:

1. Add the peas, mint, pepper, chili, honey and yogurt to a food processor and blend until smooth.
2. Meanwhile, heat a pan of water on a high heat and bring to the boil.
3. Add the zucchini noodles and turn the heat down to simmer for 3-4 minutes.
4. Remove from the heat and place in a bowl of cold water immediately.
5. Serve zucchini noodles with the pea dressing.
6. Mix the arugula with the lemon juice and serve on the side.
7. Enjoy!

(Serves 2)

Calories per serving: 219, Protein: 9g, Carbs: 18g, Fat: 12G

SCALLION & GOATS CHEESE PANCAKES

Enjoy pancakes the savoury way.

Ingredients

2 Eggs
1/2 Cup Rice Milk (Unenriched)
1/2 Cup Water
1 Tsp Black Pepper
1 Scoop Unflavored Protein Powder
1/2 Cup Rolled Oats
1 Tbsp Coconut Oil
1/4 Cup Scallions, Finely Diced
1/4 Cup Goats' Cheese, Crumbled

1 Tsp Thyme

How to make:

1. In a medium bowl add the eggs, milk, water, and pepper together until combined.
2. Add the oats and protein powder to the mix and whisk into a smooth paste.
3. Use a food processor for convenience here.
4. Take 2 tbsp of the oil and melt in a skillet over a medium heat.
5. Add 1/2 pancake mixture to form a round pancake shape.
6. Cook for 4-5 minutes until the bottom is light brown and easily comes away from the pan with the spatula.
7. Flip and add half the scallions and crumbled cheese over the top before cooking for a further 4 minutes.
8. Fold and serve warm - the cheese should have melted and the onions will be warm but still crunchy.
9. Serve and repeat with the rest of the ingredients.

(Serves 2)

Calories per serving: 334, Protein: 19g, Carbs: 23g, Fat: 16G

CHILI & HONEY SQUASH WITH CRISPY KALE & TOFU

Protein and vitamin rich.

Ingredients

1 Butternut Squash
1 Tbsp Raw Honey
1 Tbsp Chili Flakes
2 Cups Kale
4 Garlic Cloves, Whole
1 Cup Firm Tofu, Pressed

How to make:

1. Preheat the oven to 375°f/190°c/Gas Mark 5.
2. Peel and slice the butternut squash as thin as possible.
3. Layer on a lined baking dish and drizzle with honey.
4. Sprinkle chili flakes over the top and use a spatula or spoon to toss and coat thoroughly.
5. Add to the oven for 35-40 minutes.
6. Meanwhile, on a separate baking tray, layer the kale and tofu with the garlic cloves scattered on top.
7. Sprinkle with nutmeg and add to the oven for 30 minutes or until crispy.

(Serves 2)

Calories per serving: 189, Protein: 9g, Carbs: 33g, Fat: 3G

LIME & GINGER TEMPAH

Chunky tempah with a kick

Ingredients

1 Pack tempah
1 Lime, juiced
1 Tbsp ginger, grated
1 Tsp soy sauce
1 Tsp coconut oil
1 Cup sugar snap peas/edamame
1 Tsp chili flakes

How to make:

1. Mix the oil, soy sauce, lime juice and ginger and marinate the tempah for as long as possible.
2. Preheat the broiler to a medium heat.
3. Add tempah to a lined baking tray and broil for 10-15 minutes or until hot through.
4. Meanwhile, boil a pot of water over a high heat.
5. Once boiling, add the sugar snap peas/edamame to a steamer/colander over the top of the pan.
6. Lower the heat and steam for 10 minutes.
7. Remove and sprinkle with chili flakes.
8. Serve the tempah with the crunchy peas and enjoy.

(Serves 2)

Calories per serving: 247, Protein: 13g, Carbs: 25g, Fat: 15G

SIDES & SOUPS

Not enough to fill you up? Craving your side order of fries? Eyes bigger than your belly? No sweat. Here's a sweet collection of side orders you can prepare in your own home – add calories, protein and a little extra something, whilst knowing you've made it in the healthy way.

SWEET POTATO WEDGES

You won't be the only one devouring these tasty wedges.

Ingredients

4 sweet potatoes, scrubbed and cut into large wedges
2 tbsp olive oil
3-4 cloves of garlic
Handful of rosemary sprigs

How to make:

1. Pre-heat oven to (350°F/180 °C/Gas Mark 4).
2. Once you've scrubbed the skin of the sweet potatoes (don't remove it) with a kitchen scourer or something rough to suffice, you should toss the wedges in olive oil.
3. Spread these out on a baking tray, sprinkling the rosemary sprigs over the wedges and adding the whole garlic cloves in their skin over and around the wedges. Pop the whole lot into a pre-heated oven for 30-40 minutes or until crispy.

(Serves 1)

Calories per serving: 207, Protein: 3g, Carbs: 38g, Fat: 6g

HOT & SPICY BUTTERNUT SQUASH

Often ignored in our fruit and veg selection, squash is a winner! One squash will feed a family, and if you're dining solo, freeze and save for another day!.

Ingredients

1 butternut squash
4 tbsp olive oil
4 tbsp pouring honey
1 deseeded and finely chopped red scotch bonnet chilli

How to make:

1. Preheat the oven to (200°C/400°F/gas 6).
2. Chop the top and the bottom from the butternut squash. Next you need to cut it in half lengthways. You should now be able to use a vegetable peeler to remove the skin but if that doesn't work, take a sharp knife and cut downwards.
3. Now, using a spoon hollow out the seeds from the base.
4. You're free to slice now into thick (1-2 cm) slices horizontally.
5. On a lightly oiled baking tray, spread the slices into one layer across.
6. Drizzle the honey generously over the slices and sprinkle the chopped chili liberally (or according to heat tolerance!)
7. Bake for 35-40 minutes or until crispy.
8. Any left overs can be placed into a sealable sandwich bag and frozen – simply reheat in the oven when ready.

(Serves 4)

Calories per serving: 227, Protein: 1g, Carbs: 30g, Fat: 14g

FRUITY NUTTY QUINOA

Don't know what to do with your quinoa? This dish is absolutely delicious and will go great with most main meals.

Ingredients

1 1/2 cup quinoa
6 dried apricots
Juice of 1 lemon
2 tbsp olive oil
A pinch of salt and pepper
Handful of chopped parsley and mint
2oz cashew nuts

How to make:

1. Add the quinoa to a large pan of boiling water and then let simmer for 10 – 15 minutes until tender, then drain.
2. Get a bowl and add the quinoa, apricots, herbs, lemon juice, zest and olive oil along with some salt and pepper and mix together.
3. Scatter the cashews over the top and serve.

(Serves 4)

Calories per serving: 328, Protein: 10g, Carbs: 36g, Fat: 15g

RICE & PEAS

Transport yourself to the Caribbean with this easy to prepare side dish..

Ingredients

2 cups brown rice
8oz dried kidney beans
1 tsp chilli powder

How to make:

1. Soak the kidney beans in water overnight (you can buy tinned and use immediately if you're in a rush but you won't get that authentic color or taste!)
2. Boil the liquid with the kidney beans in using a large saucepan on a high heat (add water if you need to).
3. Add the rice and cook for 30 minutes and then drain. Keep the rice in the pan, add the kidney beans and cover and steam for 4 minutes.
4. Sprinkle chilli powder over your rice and serve.

(Serves 2)

Calories per serving: 430, Protein: 20g, Carbs: 16g, Fat: 15g

MUSCLE RICE SALAD

Add variety to your standard brown rice with this delicious and nutritious side.

Ingredients

1 cup of brown rice
1 deseeded and finely chopped red pepper,
½ cucumber finely chopped
1 large grated carrot
10 chopped cherry tomatoes
2 tbsp olive oil

How to make:

1. Add 1 cup of cold water to a pot and heat on high until the water is boiling.
2. Once boiling, add the rice and leave for 20 minutes. Then drain.
3. Mix the rice with chopped red pepper, chopped cucumber, grated carrot, cherry tomatoes and drizzle with olive oil

(Serves 2)

Calories per serving: 454, Protein: 11g, Carbs: 64g, Fat: 19g

LEMON AND MOROCCAN MINT COUSCOUS

A fresh and zingy side dish that works well with fish, chicken, vegetables, and even lamb and beef.

Ingredients

1.5 cup couscous
2 tbsp grated zest of a lemon and the lemon juice
pinch of fresh mint
4 tbsp toasted pine nuts

How to make:

1. In a serving bowl, pour boiling water over the dried couscous (it needs to cover the couscous with about a cm on the top) and cover the bowl with a plate to steam. You could add a chicken/vegetable stock cube to the boiling water for seasoning if you wish.
2. Once the couscous has steamed for a few minutes uncover it and use a fork to 'fluff up' the grains.
3. Add the lemon zest and juice, finely chopped mint and pine nuts.
4. Season to taste and add a little olive oil to serve.

(Serves 2)

Calories per serving: 367, Protein: 6g, Carbs: 43g, Fat: 20g

MUSHROOM RISOTTO

Another dish that works well on the side – try it with chicken breast. Works great as a post workout side!

Ingredients

2oz dried porcini mushrooms
8oz sliced and washed pack chestnut mushrooms
2 tbsp olive oil
1 finely chopped onion,
2 finely chopped garlic cloves,
2 cups risotto rice, such as Arborio
0.5 cup white wine
Handful tarragon leaves chopped
2oz freshly grated parmesan or grana padano,

How to make:

1. Pour 1 litre of boiling water over the dried porcini mushrooms and leave to soak for 20 minutes, then drain into a separate bowl (keep the liquid at this point as you need to add to the risotto later).
2. Chop the mushrooms into slices.
3. Heat up the oil on a medium heat in a large frying pan and add the onions and garlic, frying for around 5 minutes until they get soft.
4. At this point you should add the dried and fresh chestnut mushrooms and stir for another 5 minutes until softened.
5. Add the rice, stirring for a minute or so before adding all of the wine.
6. Let it get to simmering point (bubbling), and add a quarter of the mushroom stock.
7. Simmer the rice, stirring often, until the rice has absorbed all the liquid.
8. Keep adding the stock, a quarter at a time, each time waiting for the rice to absorb the liquid.
9. A lot of stirring is required until the rice is soft! If the liquid runs out and the rice is still a little hard you can continue to add small amounts of water.
10. When soft, take the pan off the heat and add half the cheese and tarragon leaves. Cover the pan and let it steam for a few minutes.
11. Serve with the rest of the cheese and herbs!

(Serves 2)

Calories per serving: 445, Protein: 15g, Carbs: 63g, Fat: 17g

BRAWNY GUACAMOLE HOUMOUS

Guacamole and houmous in one bowl – both tasty and healthy! .

Ingredients

1 can of chickpeas
1 avocado, chopped finely
1 jalapeno chopped finely
½ tsp of tabasco
1 tbsp of tahini
Pinch of cilantro, chopped
1 lime, juiced

How to make:

1. Process all the ingredients in a blender or food processor.
2. Transfer to a serving dish.

(Serves 3)

Calories per serving: 250, Protein: 10g, Carbs: 30g, Fat: 10g

MUSCLE RANCH HOUMOUS

Try this healthy houmous with a bit of an American twist; just as healthy, and tastes delicious.

Ingredients

1 can of chickpeas
1 tsp of dried parsley
1 tsp of dried dill
1/3 jar of tahini
1 garlic clove
5 tbsp of Greek yogurt

How to make:

1. Process all the ingredients in a blender or food processor.
2. Transfer to a serving dish.

(Serves 4)

Calories per serving: 130, Protein: 10g, Carbs: 19g, Fat: 1g

LEAN POTATO SALAD

A bulky side crammed with carbohydrates to continue your stamina in the gym and beyond.

Ingredients

16oz of small white potatoes, cut into pieces
8oz of low-fat plain yogurt
2 tbsp of Dijon mustard
¼ red onion, chopped finely
Pinch of salt and pepper to taste

How to make:

1. Boil water in a large pot on a high heat.
2. Cook the potatoes until tender.
3. Set aside after draining to cool down.
4. Combine Dijon mustard, plain yogurt, seasoning and red onion in a big bowl.
5. Add the cooled potatoes. Mix well.
6. Allow to chill in the refrigerator for at least 2 hours.
7. Take out of the fridge when ready to serve. Enjoy!

(Serves 4)

Calories per serving: 192, Protein: 9g, Carbs: 30g, Fat: 4g

SUPER GUACAMOLE & RED ONION QUINOA

Healthy and tasty!

Ingredients

1 diced avocado
1 cup of cooked quinoa
1 beef tomato, chopped
1/4 red onion, chopped
1 wedge of lime
2 tbsp of fresh coriander (cilantro), chopped
1 tsp of salt
1 tsp of black pepper
1 tsp of cumin

How to make:

1. Get a mixing bowl and toss in the quinoa, avocado, tomato, red onion, and cilantro. Add lime and other spices to taste.
2. Refrigerate. Best served cold

(Serves 1)

Calories per serving: 329, Protein: 9g, Carbs: 44g, Fat: 28g

WALNUT & BLUEBERRY QUINOA

A nutrient-packed side dish!

Ingredients

0.5 cup of cooked Quinoa
2oz of walnuts
2oz of blueberries
1 tsp cinnamon
2 tsp of honey

How to make:

1. Mix everything well using a spoon.

(Serves 1)

Calories per serving: 593, Protein: 16g, Carbs: 84g, Fat: 23g

KALE DIP

This vegetarian dip is creamy and delicious – but with a lot less fat than your average dip on the side.

Ingredients

1 bunch of kale
1/4 cup of spinach
1 small onion, diced finely
¼ cup of water
2 cloves of garlic, minced
3oz of low-fat Greek yogurt
2 tbsp of low-fat mayonnaise
Juice of 1 lemon
Pinch of salt & pepper

How to make:

1. Heat water, onions, kale, spinach and garlic in a large-sized saucepan over a high heat.
2. Set the heat to medium, cover and allow to cook for about 15 minutes until the water has evaporated and the kale is tender.
3. Place the mixture in a food processor and puree.
4. Get another bowl and stir the yogurt, mayonnaise, onion and lemon juice together.
5. Add the veggie puree once cool.
6. Stir some more while adding a dash of salt & pepper to taste.
7. Immediately serve.

(Serves 10)

Calories per serving: 30, Protein: 4g, Carbs: 6g, Fat: 2g

GOURMET GREEN BEANS

You can enjoy a hearty Thanksgiving dinner without fear of jeopardizing your muscle-building goals. This side dish will allow you to indulge and is packed with vitamins and iron!

Ingredients

8oz green beans
2 tsp of olive oil
1 red pepper, cut into strips
1 yellow pepper, cut into strips
½ tsp of red pepper, flaked
1 clove of garlic, finely chopped
1 tsp of sesame oil
½ tsp of salt
¼ tsp of black pepper, freshly ground
½ tsp of onion powder

How to make:

1. Drop the beans in a saucepan of boiling water.
2. Allow to cook for about 3 minutes or until the desired tenderness is achieved.
3. Drain the beans and put in cold water to prevent further cooking.
4. Get a new saucepan and fry peppers lightly in olive oil at medium heat.
5. Once softened, add green beans, garlic, red pepper flakes, salt & pepper, onion powder, and sesame oil.
6. Once spices are distributed evenly, transfer to a serving dish.
7. Serve hot

(Serves 4)

Calories per serving: 270, Protein: 4g, Carbs: 15g, Fat: 2g

BRAWNY BLACK BEAN & SWEET POTATO SIDE

Protein-packed side dish that brings a lot of flavour – especially if you love chilli!

Ingredients

6oz of black beans
6oz of cannellini beans
2 sweet potatoes, peeled & chopped
2 pieces of medium carrots, sliced
2 cloves of garlic, minced
1 piece of small onion, diced
½ piece of red bell pepper, chopped
12oz of chopped tomatoes
1/4 cup of vegetable broth
1 tbsp of chili powder
½ tsp of garlic powder
2 tbsp of olive oil
1 tsp of cumin
½ tsp of cayenne
½ tsp of salt
¼ tsp of black pepper

How to make:

1. Heat olive oil in a pan over a medium heat.
2. Sautee garlic and onions for about 1 or 2 minutes.
3. Add carrots, bell pepper, and sweet potatoes for about 6 minutes or until the onions are soft.
4. Lower heat setting to medium-low, then add the rest of the ingredients. Stir to mix well.
5. Cover partially and simmer.
6. Allow to cook for around 25 minutes, occasionally stirring until veggies are cooked, and the flavours have blended well.
7. Serve.

(Serves 2)

Calories per serving: 238, Protein: 15g, Carbs: 40g, Fat: 2g

SWEET POTATO & GREEN PEA SOUP

Fat-free and a completely vegan recipe.

Ingredients

9oz of green split peas, dried
1 large carrot, chopped
2 small sweet potatoes, chopped
1 stalk of celery, chopped
5 cups of water
½ onion, chopped
½ tsp of garlic powder
½ piece of bay leaf
½ tsp of dried oregano
½ tsp of curry powder
¼ tsp of pepper
¼ tsp of salt

How to make:

1. Combine water, split peas, onion, and other spices in a large-sized sauce pan on a medium to low heat.
2. Allow to simmer uncovered for about 1 hour.
3. Add the rest of the ingredients. Continue to simmer, this time covered, for 45 minutes more or just until the desired soup thickness is reached. Stir occasionally.
4. Remove the bay leaf.
5. Transfer everything into a blender, and process.
6. Reheat slightly before serving.

(Serves 2)

Calories per serving: 173, Protein: 6g, Carbs: 35g, Fat: 1g

MUSCLE LENTIL SOUP

You will definitely enjoy the perfect blend of spices in this very traditional warming soup! Lentils are packed with protein and goodness.

Ingredients

1/3 cup of vegetable broth
1 tsp of olive oil
1 carrot, sliced
4oz of brown lentils
1 onion, diced
2 tsp of lemon juice
2 bay leaves
Salt & pepper, to taste
¼ tsp of dried thyme

How to make:

1. Sauté carrot and onion in sunflower oil on a medium heat for around 5 minutes or until onions have become translucent.
2. Add lentils, bay leaves, thyme, salt & pepper, and vegetable broth. Lower heat and simmer. Put the lid on and allow to cook for about 40 to 45 minutes, just to make sure the lentils have softened.
3. Take the leaves out, and stir the lemon juice in.
4. Serve hot.

(Serves 2)

Calories per serving: 398, Protein: 25g, Carbs: 70g, Fat: 2g

BRAWNY BLACK BEAN SOUP

This is a tasty and easy to prepare bean soup that can get you all warmed up and ready to power on in only 15 minutes!

Ingredients

28oz of black beans, undrained
1/2 cup of vegetable broth
2oz of salsa
2 tbsp of chili powder
2 tbsp of garlic powder
2oz of cheddar cheese, shredded
1 chopped red onion
A pinch of salt and pepper

How to make:

1. Pulse half of the beans in food processor with a bit of water until smooth.
2. Put all beans in a medium-sized saucepan. Add salsa, chilli powder, and vegetable broth. Bring to a boil on a high heat. Top with cheese and onions.
3. Serve and enjoy!

(Serves 4)

Calories per serving: 231, Protein: 18g, Carbs: 43g, Fat: 5g

CARROT, QUINOA & TARRAGON SOUP

A real zingy soup – great for winter but can be served cooled in the summer too!

Ingredients

2 Tbsp olive oil
1 Tsp mustard seeds, ground
1 Tsp fennel seeds, ground
1 Tbsp tarragon
1 Tbsp ginger, minced
1 Cup quinoa
1 Onion, chopped
6 Carrots, peeled & chopped
Zest and juice of 1 orange
3 Cups low-salt vegetable stock/
Chicken stock/water
Black pepper to taste
3 Cups of water

How to make:

1. In a pan on a medium heat, add the oil.
2. Once hot, add the seeds for 1 minute.
3. Add the ginger and cook for a further minute.
4. Then add the carrots, onions and the orange juice, cooking for at least 5 minutes or until the vegetables are soft.
5. Add the stock and tarragon and bring to the boil before turning the heat down slightly.
6. Add the quinoa to the pan and simmer for 30 minutes.
7. Allow to cool.
8. Put the mixture in a food processor and puree until smooth (leave some lumps for a chunky soup).
9. Serve with orange zest and black pepper

(Serves 4)

Calories per serving: 589, Protein: 26g, Carbs: 71g, Fat: 29g

SPAGHETTI SQUASH & YELLOW LENTIL SOUP

The lentils add a protein hit to this soup.

Ingredients

1 Spaghetti squash, peeled and cubed
4 Cups low-salt vegetable stock/
Chicken stock/water
1 Tbsp coconut oil
1 Onion, quartered and sliced
2 Large garlic cloves, chopped
1 Sprig of thyme/1 tbsp dried thyme
1 Cup yellow lentils
1 Tsp curry powder

How to make:

1. Heat oil in a large pan over a medium high heat before sweating the onions and garlic for 3-4 minutes.
2. Add the stock and bring to a boil over a high heat before adding the squash and lentils.
3. Turn down heat and allow to simmer for 25-30 minutes.
4. Now add the rest of the ingredients and simmer for a further 15 minutes or until the squash is tender.
5. Serve hot!

(Serves 2)

Calories per serving: 278, Protein: 19g, Carbs: 29g, Fat: 15g

RED PEPPER & PINTO BEAN SOUP

Adding beans to your soup adds a delicious texture and extra goodness!

Ingredients

8 Red bell peppers, chopped
1 Red onion, chopped
2 Garlic cloves, chopped
3 Cups chicken/veg stock
2 Cup pinto beans, canned
2 Tbsp of extra virgin olive oil
1 Tsp cumin
1 Tsp paprika

How to make:

1. In a pan on a medium heat, heat the oil then add the onions and peppers, sweating for 5 minutes.
2. Add the garlic cloves, cumin and paprika and saute for 3-4 minutes.
3. Add the broth and allow to boil before turning heat down slightly.
4. Add the pinto beans and simmer for 30 minutes.
5. Remove from the heat and allow to cool slightly.
6. Put the mixture in a food processor and puree until smooth or leave for a chunky soup.
7. Season with black pepper to serve.

(Serves 4)

Calories per serving: 494, Protein: 13g, Carbs: 26g, Fat: 13g

CHICKEN & LEMONGRASS SOUP

This chunky soup with asian style broth is a must!

Ingredients

1 Tbsp coconut oil
1 Tbsp cilantro
1 Cup mushrooms
1 Fresh lime
1 Garlic clove, minced
1 Thumb size piece of minced ginger
1 White onion, chopped
1/2 Cup pak choi/bok choy
A handful of fresh basil leaves
1/2 Cup of chicken broth
1/2 Cup of coconut milk
1 Green chili, finely chopped
2 Stems of green onion, chopped
4X skinless chicken breasts, sliced
1/2 Stick lemongrass, sliced

How to make:

1. Crush the lemongrass, cilantro, chili, 1 tbsp oil and basil leaves in a blender or pestle and mortar to form a paste.
2. Heat a large pan/wok with 1 tbsp olive oil on a high heat.
3. Sauté the onions, garlic and ginger until soft.
4. Add the chicken and brown each side.
5. Add the coconut milk and stir. Now add the paste.
6. Slowly add the stock until a broth is formed.
7. Now add the mushrooms, turn down the heat slightly and allow to simmer for 25-30 minutes or until chicken is thoroughly cooked through.
8. Add the bok choy 5 minutes before the end of the cooking time.
9. Serve hot with the green onion sprinkled over the top.

(Serves 4)

Calories per serving: 254, Protein: 33g, Carbs: 19g, Fat: 12g

CURRIED CHICKPEA & GARLIC SOUP

Chickpeas are a great way of adding protein to your meal.

Ingredients

2 Tbsp coconut oil
4 Cloves garlic, minced
1/2 Cauliflower, chopped
2 Onions, peeled and chopped
1 Cup chickpeas, canned
1 Tsp cumin
1 Tsp turmeric
3 Cups water
1 Cup homemade chicken stock
1 Cup low fat coconut milk

How to make:

1. Heat the oil in a large pan over a medium high heat.
2. Add the onions, garlic and cauliflower and sweat for 5-10 minutes (don't let them brown).
3. Add the chickpeas and spices and cook for another 5 minutes.
4. Add the stock and bring to a boil before lowering heat and simmering for 15-20 minutes.
5. Remove from heat and allow to cool before blending in a food processor or liquidizer. Alternatively enjoy chunky and skip step 5.
6. Return to the pan and add the coconut milk, warming through.
7. Serve with a sprinkle of black pepper.

(Serves 4)

Calories per serving: 434, Protein: 17g, Carbs: 45g, Fat: 24g

NUTMEG, SPINACH & PORK SOUP

Tasty.

Ingredients

1 Tbsp extra-virgin olive oil
1 Tbsp ground nutmeg
1 Cup chicken or vegetable stock
6Oz lean ground pork
1 Onion, chopped
2 Cups spinach
2 Garlic cloves, minced
1 Tsp black pepper

How to make:

1. In a large pot, add the oil, chopped onion and minced garlic, sautéing for 5 minutes on low heat.
2. Add the pork to the onions and cook for 7-8 minutes or until browned.
3. Add the stock to the pan and bring to a boil on a high heat.
4. Stir in the spinach, reduce heat and simmer for a further 20 minutes or until pork thoroughly cooked through.
5. Allow to cool slightly and add to a food processor until smooth.
6. Season with pepper to serve.

(Serves 2)

Calories per serving: 286, Protein: 22g, Carbs: 7g, Fat: 27g

WHITE BEAN & MED VEG SOUP

Hearty, chunky soup.

Ingredients

1 Tbsp extra-virgin olive oil
1 Tbsp oregano
2 Cups chicken or vegetable stock
1 Cup white beans, canned
1 Onion, chopped
1 Zucchini, finely chopped
1 Eggplant, finely chopped
1 Red pepper, finely chopped
2 Garlic cloves, minced
1 Tsp black pepper

How to make:

1. In a large pot, add the oil, chopped onion and minced garlic, sautéing for 5 minutes on low heat.
2. Add the other vegetables to the onions and cook for 7-8 minutes or until browned.
3. Add the stock to the pan and bring to a boil on a high heat.
4. Stir in the herbs and beans, reduce heat and simmer for a further 20 minutes or until thoroughly cooked through.
5. Season with pepper to serve.

(Serves 2)

Calories per serving: 326, Protein: 20g, Carbs: 38g, Fat: 14g

HEALTHY VEGETABLE STOCK

Use as a healthy alternative to shop bought stocks.

Ingredients

2 Onions
3 Carrots
3 Celery stalks
1 Garlic clove
1 Tbsp extra virgin olive oil
1 Bay leaf
1 Tbsp thyme
1 Tbsp parsley
1 Tsp black peppercorns

How to make:

1. Peel and chop vegetables and soak in warm water.
2. Heat the oil in a large pot over a medium heat and add the vegetables, garlic, herbs and peppercorns, cooking for 5 minutes.
3. Fill up the pot with boiling water.
4. Turn up the heat and bring to the boil - allow to simmer for 25 minutes.
5. Strain stock and use immediately or allow to cool and refrigerate for 2-3 days or freeze for 3-4 weeks in a sealed container.

(Serves 2)

Calories per serving: 5, Protein: 1g, Carbs: 1g, Fat: 0g

LEAN CHICKEN STOCK

Use as a healthy alternative to shop bought stocks..

Ingredients

1 Whole roasting chicken {around 4-5lbs}
3 Carrots, soaked in warm water
2 Medium onions
4 Garlic cloves, crushed
2 Bay leaves
3 Stalks of celery, soaked in warm water
1 Tbsp each dried rosemary, thyme, pepper, turmeric
1 Tbsp white wine vinegar
11-12 Cups water

How to make:

1. Rinse off your chicken and place in a large saucepan or soup pan (remove giblets but don't waste them; add them in to your stock bowl!)
2. Chop your vegetables into large chunks (quarters at the smallest). Leave the skins on as they add to the taste and the nutrients - add to the pan.
3. Add the herbs, spices and pepper to the pan.
4. Fill your pan with water so that the chicken and vegetables are completely covered.
5. Turn stove on high and bring to boiling point before reducing the heat and allowing the stock to simmer for 3-4 hours.
6. Check at intervals and top up with water if the ingredients become uncovered.
7. Take off the heat and carefully remove the chicken, placing to one side.
8. You now need to strain the liquid from the stockpot into another bowl using a sieve to get rid of all the lumpy bits.
9. Leave the stock and chicken to cool.
10. Once cool, tear or cut the meat from the bones.
11. Once the stock has cooled to room temperature,

add to a sealed container and keep in the fridge.

12. Save the chicken for a delicious salad or to add back into the stock to make a chunky chicken soup.

13. The stock can be kept for 3 days in the fridge/3 months in freezer in an airtight Tupperware box or Kilner jar - just skim off the fat when ready to use.

(Serves 2)

Calories per serving: 71, Protein: 9g, Carbs: 2g, Fat: 7g

SALADS

Salads are boring right? They're only designed for rabbits and skinny women on diets. Wrong. Salads done right are firstly delicious and don't have to just be a side; secondly they can be stuffed with fibre, protein, vitamins, and nutrients. Don't make the stupid error of ignoring our age-old, trusted training companions and try a super strong salad soon.

MEDITERRANEAN SUPER SALAD

Quinoa's goodness cannot be overstated, this salad is packed full of protein and is also delicious too!

Ingredients

1.5 cup quinoa
1 tsp olive oil
½ red onion, finely chopped
2 tbsp mint (fresh or dried) and roughly chopped
16oz of Puy or Red lentils rinsed and drained – you can buy the dried lentils but you need to leave them to soak over night.
¼ cucumber (skin off and diced)
4oz crumbled feta cheese
Zest and juice of 1 orange
1 tbsp red or white wine vinegar

How to make:

1. Cook the quinoa in a large pan of boiling water for 10-15 minutes until soft, drain and set aside to cool.
2. Fry the onion in the oil over a medium heat.
3. Stir together with the quinoa, lentils, cucumber, feta, orange zest, chopped mint and juice and vinegar.
4. Best served chilled!
5. For the meat fans, cooked chicken or lamb would be a delicious addition to this dish!

(Serves 1)

Calories per serving: 290, Protein: 15g, Carbs: 35g, Fat: 10g

HUNKED UP HALLOUMI

This cheese could almost be meat it's so chunky and filling!

Ingredients

2 tbsp white wine vinegar
2 tsp olive oil
½ red onion thinly sliced
Handful of rocket leaves
½ juiced lemon
Handful of green/black olives
16oz of sliced halloumi cheese
1 tbsp mayonnaise
½ chopped cucumber
A pinch of pepper

How to make:

1. Preheat the grill.
2. Lightly drizzle a baking tray with 1 tsp olive oil before grilling for 5 minutes, turning until browned and crisp on the edges.
3. Add the chopped olives, rocket, cucumber and red onion into a bowl and mix with 1 tsp olive oil and lemon juice.
4. Season with pepper and stir in the mayonnaise (optional).
5. Serve alone or with crusty brown pitta breads for an Aegean twist!

(Serves 4)

Calories per serving: 461, Protein: 29g, Carbs: 3g, Fat: 37g

ROASTED BEETROOT, GOATS' CHEESE & EGG SALAD

Whether you love it or hate it, beetroot is a super food containing nutrients you rarely find in your five portions a day! Give it a go if you never have, or try this take on it if you're already a fan

Ingredients

8oz cooked chopped beetroot (not in vinegar)
2 tbsp olive oil
Juice from 1 orange
2 eggs
1 tsp white wine vinegar
2 tbsp crème fraîche
1 tsp Dijon mustard
A few stalks of dill, finely chopped (fresh or dried)
1 cup of baby gem lettuce
Handful of walnuts
4oz crumbled goats cheese
A pinch of salt and pepper

How to make:

1. Preheat oven to (200°C/400°F/Gas Mark 6).
2. Place the beetroot onto the lightly oiled baking tray with the juice from the orange, sprinkle with salt and pepper.
3. Roast for 20-25 minutes, turning them once whilst they're baking. If they start to dry out, add a little more olive oil.
4. Meanwhile, put the eggs in boiling water. Turn down the heat and simmer for 8 minutes (4 minutes if you like your yolks runny) then run under cold water to cool. Peel and halve.
5. Mix the remaining oil, crème fraîche, mustard, a tsp of white wine vinegar and chopped dill together. This is the dressing for your lettuce.
6. Serve the salad with the beetroot and goats cheese crumbled over the top and walnuts sprinkled throughout

(Serves 1)

Calories per serving: 363, Protein: 11g, Carbs: 18g, Fat: 28g

SPICY MEXICAN BEAN STEW

This one is technically a salad but really it could pass on anyone's dinner table. You won't be left hungry after this one and you'll certainly feel the heat kick-starting your metabolism!

Ingredients

8oz canned chick peas, drained
8oz canned cannellini beans, drained
8oz of tinned chopped tomatoes
2 tbsp olive oil
1 chopped red onion
6oz of sliced chorizo
3 red chopped chillis
1 tbsp paprika

How to make:

1. Heat a large pan on a medium heat with 1 tbsp olive oil, and cook the onion and chorizo for 5 minutes until lightly golden.
2. Tip in the chickpeas with the cannellini beans and stir until heated through.
3. Add the tin of chopped tomatoes and paprika and cover to let simmer for 5-10 minutes.
4. Serve – recommended with crusty brown bread, couscous or brown rice for a winter warmer!

(Serves 4)

Calories per serving: 395, Protein: 20g, Carbs: 45g, Fat: 15g

THE SAILOR SALAD

Spinach was good enough for the well-known muscle-building sailor cartoon then and its more than good enough for you now; add a generous portion of the sailor's catch and you'll be growing bigger than he ever did.

Ingredients

1 bag of chopped spinach (fresh)
8oz of lean grilled chopped turkey breast (or turkey deli meat already cooked)
1 tbsp real bacon bits (you can cut up bacon and grill this yourself or buy the pre-packaged stuff)
2 diced hard-boiled eggs
4oz baby potatoes
1 deseeded and sliced red, yellow and green pepper
1 avocado peeled and sliced (do this near to the end or it will start to turn brown)
1 tbsp balsamic vinegar
A pinch of salt and pepper

How to make:

1. Boil a medium sized pan of water on a high heat and add the halved new potatoes, cooking for 15-20 minutes or according to packaging guidelines.
2. Combine the meats (once grilled and chopped if you're doing this yourself) with the spinach and peppers in a serving bowl.
3. Drain the potatoes and let cool whilst placing a small pan to boil for the eggs. Cook for 8 minutes for medium-boiled or 10 minutes for hard-boiled eggs.
4. Run the eggs under a cold tap and peel. Dice and add to your salad (here's where you can peel the avocado and add this).
5. Stir through with balsamic vinegar and salt and pepper to taste.

(Serves 4)

Calories per serving: 220, Protein: 20g, Carbs: 13g, Fat: 10g

SIZZLING SALMON SALAD

Some like it hot. You can serve this one up with warm or cold salmon – either way it's wholesome and mouth-watering.

Ingredients

6oz fillet salmon
6 cherry tomatoes
1 cup of couscous
3 stems of asparagus (chop off the very end of the base but leave the rest intact)
2oz of diced low-fat mozzarella cheese
1 bell pepper sliced
1 tbsp balsamic vinegar
1 tbsp olive oil
A pinch of salt and pepper

How to make:

1. Preheat the grill.
2. Layer the couscous with boiling water from the kettle (about 1cm over the top of the couscous, cover and leave to steam)
3. Grill salmon for 10-15 minutes or until cooked through. Place to one side.
4. Uncover the couscous and stir through with a fork to break up the grains.
5. Now just add your pepper, mozzarella and halved cherry tomatoes to the couscous.
6. You will need to grill your asparagus for 3-4 minutes, turning every so often until lightly browned around the surface.
7. Once the asparagus is ready, place it along with the salmon on the bed of couscous and drizzle with olive oil and balsamic vinegar.
8. Salt and pepper to taste.

(Serves 1)

Calories per serving: 521, Protein: 46g, Carbs: 24g, Fat: 27g

HERBY TUNA STEAK

Protein, protein, protein! .

Ingredients

2x 8oz dolphin-friendly yellow fin tuna steaks
1 tbsp olive oil
2 lemon wedges
2 handfuls of flat-leaf parsley and 2 handfuls of coriander very roughly chopped
2 cloves of finely chopped garlic
½ onion finely chopped
Handful chopped green olives
6 tbsp olive oil
2oz pine nuts or walnuts
Juice of half a lemon

How to make:

1. Your first job is the herby salad – mix the herbs with half of the chopped garlic, lemon juice and olive oil.
2. Crush the nuts in a tea towel or blend them up in your blender. Stir them in to the herbs.
3. Brush the tuna steaks with olive oil and sprinkle with salt and pepper.
4. You need to heat dry pan to an extremely high heat (look out for the smoke)
5. Seal the tuna in the pan for one minute on each side (if you have a griddle pan or grill then you should place these against the lines to get that nice straight off the BBQ look and taste)
6. If you like your tuna less-pink cook for 2 minutes on each side for medium, 3 for medium well and 4 for well done (approximate times).
7. Once cooked serve straight away with your herby salad (pour this over as a dressing or on the side as an accompaniment)

(Serves 2)

Calories per serving: 578, Protein: 35g, Carbs: 3g, Fat: 48g

MUSCLE BUILDING STEAK & CHEESE SALAD

A very quick and easy, healthy muscle building salad.

Ingredients

8oz frying beef steak
1 chopped red onion
1 teaspoon of crushed garlic
Handful of baby spinach
Handful of watercress
Handful of lettuce
4 chopped baby tomatoes
2 tbsp of balsamic vinegar
1 tbsp olive oil
2oz of blue cheese
A pinch of salt and pepper

How to make:

1. Sprinkle salt and pepper over the steak.
2. Add a tbsp of olive oil to a griddle pan on a high heat.
3. Place the steak in the pan and cook 8 minutes in total, turning the steak half way through. Take the steak off the pan and allow to cool.
4. Cut the steak into 2cm strips, then place back into the pan and cook for a further minute on a medium heat.
5. Get a bowl and add the chopped tomatoes, watercress, baby spinach, lettuce, garlic and onions. Place the steak strips in the bowl along with the vinegar and a tbsp of olive oil. Mix everything together and grate the blue cheese over the top.

(Serves 2)

Calories per serving: 308, Protein: 34g, Carbs: 15g, Fat: 14g

ANABOLIC AVOCADO AND CHICKEN SALAD

A fresh and delicious salad, pleasing the meat eater and keeping you anabolic!

Ingredients

1 chicken breast
Handful of watercress
Handful of baby spinach
Handful of rocket
½ peeled and sliced avocado
1 chopped beef tomato
¼ sliced cucumber
2 tbsp of olive oil

How to make:

1. Heat some olive oil on a medium heat in a griddle pan.
2. Grill the chicken breast for about 10 minutes each side or until cooked through.
3. Cut the chicken breasts into chunks and serve with the watercress, spinach, rocket, tomato and sliced avocado.
4. Finish off the salad by drizzling over olive oil.

(Serves 1)

Calories per serving: 389, Protein: 36g, Carbs: 12g, Fat: 14g

STRENGTH CHICKEN AND SESAME SALAD

Contains three sources of protein for all your muscle-building needs.

Ingredients

2 chicken breasts
3 tbsp of sesame oil
2 tsp of grated ginger
1 crushed garlic clove
1 chopped red chilli
1 diced red onion
Handful of basil leaves
Handful of coriander leaves
1 cup of baby spinach leaves
1 tsp of sesame seeds
4 chopped almonds
1 peeled and sliced mandarin

How to make:

1. Pre-heat the grill.
2. Add 2 tbsp sesame oil, chopped red chilli, crushed garlic and ginger into a bowl. Mix all the ingredients together.
3. Make a few deep cuts into the chicken breast and leave them to marinate in the mixture for roughly 3 hours.
4. Add the spinach leaves, coriander leaves, basil leaves, red onion, chopped almonds and sesame seeds to a bowl and mix together.
5. Remove the chicken and rub over the last of the marinade and grill for 10 minutes each side or until fully cooked.
6. Cut the chicken into strips and add to the salad bowl.
7. Add the mandarin to the bowl and drizzle 1 tbsp of sesame oil over the salad and serve

(Serves 2)

Calories per serving: 430, Protein: 20g, Carbs: 16g, Fat: 15g

TUNA & SUPER SPINACH SALAD

Quick and easy tasty tuna salad for your muscle building and fat loss needs..

Ingredients

2x 4oz cans of tinned tuna in olive oil
Handful of baby spinach
1 chopped red onion
2 chopped red or green peppers
1 tbsp olive oil
1 chopped red chilli
10 halved cherry tomatoes
Handful of chopped black olives
½ iceberg lettuce chopped into slices

How to make:

1. Get a bowl and mix all of the ingredients apart from the lettuce together before tossing and drizzling with olive oil.
2. Layer the salad onto your plate before topping with the tuna mixture.
3. Serve and enjoy.

(Serves 2)

Calories per serving: 302, Protein: 18g, Carbs: 28g, Fat: 13g

THE SWEET SAILOR SALAD

Spinach was good enough for the well-known muscle-building sailor cartoon then and its more than good enough for you now; add a generous portion of the sailor's catch and you'll be growing bigger than he ever did..

Ingredients

1 cup raw spinach leaves
7oz lean grilled chopped turkey breast
1 tbsp grilled real bacon bits
2 eggs (free range)
4oz of chopped sweet potatoes
1 deseeded and sliced red, yellow and green pepper
1 avocado peeled and sliced (do this near to the end or it will start to turn brown)
Sprinkle of salt and pepper

How to make:

1. Bring a pan of water to the boil on a high heat and add the chopped potatoes.
2. Cook for 15-20 minutes or according to packaging guidelines.
3. Combine the cooked meats with the spinach and peppers.
4. Drain the potatoes and leave to cool whilst placing a small pan of water to boil for the eggs.
5. Add the eggs once boiling and cook for 8 minutes for a medium-boiled and 10 minutes for a hard-boiled egg.
6. Run the eggs under a cold tap and peel.
7. Chop in half and add to your salad (here's where you can peel the avocado and add this).
8. Stir through your choice of olive oil, red/white wine vinegar and salt and pepper to taste.

(Serves 4)

Calories per serving: 220, Protein: 20g, Carbs: 13g, Fat: 10g

MUSCLE BUILDING STEAK & BALSAMIC SPINACH SALAD

A very quick and easy, healthy muscle building salad.

Ingredients

8oz frying beef steak
1 chopped red onion
1 tsp of crushed garlic
1/4 cup baby spinach
1/4 cup watercress
4 cherry tomatoes, halved
2 tbsp of balsamic vinegar
2 tbsp olive oil
Sprinkle of salt and pepper

How to make:

1. Sprinkle salt and pepper over steak.
2. Add a tbsp of olive oil to a griddle pan and heat on a high temperature.
3. Place the steak in the pan and cook for 8 minutes in total, turning the steak half way through.
4. Remove the steak from the pan and rest for 3 minutes.
5. Cut it into 2cm strips.
6. Get a bowl and add the chopped tomatoes, watercress, baby spinach, garlic and onions.
7. Place the steak strips in the bowl along with the vinegar and a tbsp of olive oil. Mix together.
8. Plate up and serve.

(Serves 2)

Calories per serving: 308, Protein: 34g, Carbs: 15g, Fat: 14g

PROTEIN PACKED EGG & BEAN SALAD

A classic American dish cooked with three kinds of beans. It is nutrient-packed as well!

Ingredients

16oz of cooked black beans, drained & rinsed
16oz of cooked cannellini beans, drained & rinsed
16oz of cooked kidney beans, drained & rinsed
6 hard-boiled eggs, sliced
1 celery stick chopped
½ onion, chopped
Handful of olives, sliced
3 tsp of hot pepper sauce
½ tsp of salt
¼ tsp of pepper
3 tsp of Italian salad dressing

How to make:

1. Drain the beans, then rinse, and finally drain again.
2. Combine celery, olives, onions, salad dressing, seasonings, and beans. Carefully mix. Refrigerate for at least 2 hours, preferably overnight.
3. When ready to serve. Drain off the salad dressing first, then add eggs.
4. Carefully mix so as not to mash the beans.
5. Serve.

(Serves 8)

Calories per serving: 366, Protein: 15g, Carbs: 30g, Fat: 14g

BULGUR WHEAT, FETA CHEESE & QUINOA SALAD

A variation of the traditional tabbouleh salad, this version features feta cheese that provides for a tasty twist, without compromising on nutrients.

Ingredients

1/2 cup of bulgur wheat, uncooked
1/2 cup of cooked quinoa
16oz of chickpeas, drained
2oz of feta cheese, crumbled
1 cup cherry tomatoes, chopped
½ jar of pesto
3 tbsp of fresh lemon juice
2 tbsp of fresh parsley, minced
1/4 tsp of black pepper
1 onion, sliced thinly
2 cups of water, boiling

How to make:

1. Mix bulgur wheat with boiling water in a large-sized bowl. Cover and set aside for half an hour before draining.
2. Add lemon juice and pesto. Stir using a whisk.
3. Combine pesto mixture, bulgur, quinoa, feta, tomatoes, green onions, chickpeas, pepper, parsley in a large bowl. Gently toss to mix well.
4. Serve

(Serves 4)

Calories per serving: 350, Protein: 15g, Carbs: 50g, Fat: 15g

HOMEMADE PROTEIN SHAKES

If you want to spend hundreds of pounds on pre-made shakes full of chemicals and fillers that cements onto your kitchen sink then be my guest! If not, try these homemade healthy alternatives that will pack on just as much punch as the shop-bought varieties.

GREEN & MEAN

Begin your day with this easy to prepare veggie-rich breakfast that packs a monstrous protein-powered punch. Go Green!

Ingredients

3 stalks of Celery
3 bunches of Kale
½ cup of sliced pineapple
½ apple, chopped
A handful of spinach
1 tbsp of coconut oil
1 scoop of vanilla protein powder

How to make:

1. Place all the ingredients together in the blender and process until the desired consistency is achieved.
2. Pour contents of the blender into a tall glass. Serve immediately and enjoy!

(Serves 1)

Calories per serving: 497, Protein: 28g, Carbs: 62g, Fat: 17g

CHOCOLATE PEANUT DELIGHT

Get your chocolate fix with this tasty shake.

Ingredients

1 scoop of chocolate whey protein powder
1 cup of low-fat Greek yogurt
1 whole banana
2 tbsp of peanut butter
1 cup of ice

How to make:

1. Add all the ingredients to a blender and blend until smooth.
2. Enjoy.

(Serves 1)

Calories per serving: 656, Protein: 63g, Carbs: 55g, Fat: 21g

JASON'S HOMEMADE MASS GAINER

It can be hard to get in the necessary calories to grow. Most weight gainers contain empty calories and can be expensive. This beast of a shake contains around 1000 healthy calories and a whopping 75g of Protein to keep you growing..

Ingredients

2 scoop of chocolate whey protein powder
2 cups of whole milk
½ cup of dry rolled oats
1 whole banana
2 tbsp of organic almond butter
1 cup of crushed ice

How to make:

1. Add all the ingredients to a blender and blend until smooth.
2. Enjoy.

(Serves 1)

Calories per serving: 970, Protein: 75g, Carbs: 90g, Fat: 30g

BERRY PROTEIN SHAKE

Totally refreshing on a hot summer's day and it works well any time of the year...

Ingredients

2 scoop of whey protein powder
1 cup of blueberries
1 cup of blackberries
1 cup of raspberries
1 cup of water
1 cup of ice

How to make:

1. Add all the ingredients to a blender and blend until smooth.
2. Enjoy.

(Serves 1)

Calories per serving: 342, Protein: 38g, Carbs: 42g, Fat: 3g

FRESH STRAWBERRY SHAKE

Keep it simple with this strawberry shake all year round.

Ingredients

2 scoops of vanilla protein powder
1 cup of strawberries
2 cups of water
1 tbsp of flaxseed oil

How to make:

1. Add all the ingredients to a blender and blend until smooth.
2. Enjoy.

(Serves 1)

Calories per serving: 303, Protein: 35g, Carbs: 15g, Fat: 11g

CHOCO COFFEE ENERGY SHAKE

Swap your average morning caffeine hit with this refreshing alternative.

Ingredients

2 scoops of chocolate protein powder
l cup of low-fat milk
1 cup of water
1 tbsp of instant coffee

How to make:

1. Add all the ingredients to a blender and blend until smooth.
2. Enjoy.

(Serves 1)

Calories per serving: 299, Protein: 42g, Carbs: 14g, Fat: 6g

LEAN AND MEAN PINEAPPLE SHAKE

Fresh, tropical and zingy – this shake really packs a punch and is crammed full with energy to keep you going until at least lunchtime.

Ingredients

1 cup chopped fresh pineapple
4 strawberries
1 banana
1 tbsp low-fat Greek yogurt
1 scoop of vanilla protein powder
1 cup of water

How to make:

1. Add all the ingredients to a blender and blend until smooth.
2. Enjoy.

(Serves 1)

Calories per serving: 355, Protein: 23g, Carbs: 65g, Fat: 3g

CHOPPED ALMOND SMOOTHIE

Quick and easy shake which will satisfy your chocolate craving and provide you with 24 grams of protein.

Ingredients

1 1/2 cups water
17 chopped almonds
1/2 tsp coconut extract
1 scoop chocolate protein powder

How to make:

1. Add all the ingredients to a blender and blend until smooth.
2. Enjoy.

(Serves 1)

Calories per serving: 241, Protein: 24g, Carbs: 6g, Fat: 13g

VANILLA STRAWBERRY SURPRISE

If this doesn't transport you back to a day out by the seaside nothing will – it tastes amazing and is deceptively good at filling you up and helping you to bulk up and shred fat..

Ingredients

2 scoops of vanilla protein powder
1 cup of ice
1 banana
4 fresh or frozen strawberries

How to make:

1. Add all the ingredients to a blender and blend until smooth.
2. Enjoy.

(Serves 1)

Calories per serving: 329, Protein: 36g, Carbs: 42g, Fat: 2g

BREAKFAST BANANA SHAKE

Not much time? This breakfast shake packs a punch and will ensure a positive start to your day.

Ingredients

1 cup low-fat milk
1 banana
1 cup of rolled oats
2 scoops of vanilla whey protein powder

How to make:

1. Add all the ingredients to a blender and blend until smooth.
2. Enjoy.

(Serves 1)

Calories per serving: 566, Protein: 59g, Carbs: 69g, Fat: 6g

PEACHY PUNCH

This peachy punch will satisfy your sweet tooth as well as provide 50 grams of protein.

Ingredients

2 scoop of vanilla protein powder
1/2 cup of low-fat milk
1/2 cup of rolled oats
1 chopped peach
1 cup of water
2oz of low fat Greek yogurt

How to make:

1. Add all the ingredients to a blender and blend until smooth.
2. Enjoy.

(Serves 1)

Calories per serving: 543, Protein: 50g, Carbs: 57g, Fat: 11g

BLACKBERRY BRAWN

Quick and easy shake that is as tasty as it is nutritious.

Ingredients

1 cup of blackberries
1/2 cup of low–fat milk
1 tbsp of flax seed oil
2oz of low-fat Greek yogurt
2 scoops of vanilla protein powder
1 cup of ice

How to make:

1. Add all the ingredients to a blender and blend until smooth.
2. Enjoy.

(Serves 1)

Calories per serving: 457, Protein: 47g, Carbs: 30g, Fat: 16g

NO WHEY!

No protein powder? This healthy, tasty shake contains a nice dose of protein to keep you growing!

Ingredients

1 cup of blackberries
1 cup of strawberries
1/2 cup of low–fat milk
8oz of Greek yogurt
1 tbsp of almond butter
1 cup of ice

How to make:

1. Add all the ingredients to a blender and blend until smooth.
2. Enjoy.

(Serves 1)

Calories per serving: 388, Protein: 26g, Carbs: 32g, Fat: 22g

CARIBBEAN CRUSH

Absolutely delicious!

Ingredients

1 scoop of protein powder (your choice)
1/2 chopped mango
1/2 cup of pineapple chunks
1 peeled and cubed kiwi
1 strawberry
1 cup of ice cubes

How to make:

1. Add all the ingredients to a blender and blend until smooth.
2. Enjoy.

(Serves 1)

Calories per serving: 263, Protein: 25g, Carbs: 38g, Fat: 3g

CHOCOLATE & RASPBERRY BANG

A tasty, quick protein shake to keep you growing and shredding!

Ingredients

2 scoops of chocolate protein powder
1/2 cup of raspberries
1/2 cup of whole milk
1/2 cup of ice cubes

How to make:

1. Add all the ingredients to a blender and blend until smooth.
2. Enjoy.

(Serves 1)

Calories per serving: 269, Protein: 31g, Carbs: 16g, Fat: 9g

CINNAMON SURPRISE

Quick and easy protein shake to satisfy your taste buds, especially for a festive taste!

Ingredients

2 scoops of chocolate protein powder
1 tbsp of cinnamon
1 cup of water
1 cup of ice

How to make:

1. Add all the ingredients to a blender and blend until smooth.
2. Enjoy.

(Serves 1)

Calories per serving: 244, Protein: 47g, Carbs: 7g, Fat: 4g

PUMPKIN POWER

A great tasting shake, packed full of protein!

Ingredients

2 scoops of vanilla protein powder
1 cup of chopped pumpkin
1 tsp cinnamon
1 cup of water

How to make:

1. Add all the ingredients to a blender and blend until smooth.
2. Enjoy.

(Serves 1)

Calories per serving: 224, Protein: 38g, Carbs: 14g, Fat: 3g

LIME POWER SHAKE

Bursting with Vitamin C goodness, this power shake is packed with muscle building protein as well!

Ingredients

2 scoops of vanilla protein powder
1 piece of banana
1 cup of almond milk, unsweetened
1 tbsp of key lime juice
1 key lime zest
1 tbsp of non-fat Greek yogurt
1 tbsp of crushed graham crackers
1 cup of ice cubes
½ tsp of maple syrup

How to make:

1. Add all the ingredients to a blender and blend until smooth.
2. Enjoy.

(Serves 1)

Calories per serving: 350, Protein: 32g, Carbs: 52g, Fat: 6g

CHOCOLATE & BERRY SHAKE

Delicious pre or post workout shake!

Ingredients

2 Scoops chocolate protein powder
1/8 Cup mixed berries (frozen)
1 Tsp goji berries
1/8 Cup spinach
1/2 Cup almond milk

How to make:

1. Add all the ingredients to a blender and blend until smooth.
2. Enjoy.

(Serves 2)

Calories per serving: 214, Protein: 28g, Carbs: 19g, Fat: 2g

BRILLIANT BANANA SHAKE

Tropical smoothie!

Ingredients

1 Banana
1/8 Cup kale
1/2 Apple, sliced
1 Tsp flaxseed
1/2 Cup water
2 Scoops vanilla protein powder

How to make:

1. Add all the ingredients to a blender and blend until smooth.
2. Enjoy.

(Serves 2)

Calories per serving: 216, Protein: 25g, Carbs: 21g, Fat: 5g

TANGERINE TWIST

Packed with Vitamin C!

Ingredients

5 Tangerines
1/8 Cup spinach
Icecubes
1/2 Cup water
1 Tsp basil leaves

How to make:

1. Add all the ingredients to a blender and blend until smooth.
2. Enjoy.

(Serves 2)

Calories per serving: 121, Protein: 4g, Carbs: 27g, Fat: 1g

POWER PROTEIN SHAKE

Healthy fats and protein make this a between meal fave!

Ingredients

2 Tbsp greek yogurt
1 Scoop rolled oats
1 Tbsp almonds
1 Tsp raw honey
1 Scoop vanilla protein
1/8 Cup frozen raspberries

How to make:

1. Add all the ingredients to a blender and blend until smooth.
2. Enjoy.

(Serves 1)

Calories per serving: 440, Protein: 4g, Carbs: 33g, Fat: 10g

IMMUNE BOOST

Beat the common cold with this tasty juice

Ingredients

1 Orange, juiced
2 Peaches, peeled and sliced
1/4 Carrot, peeled and sliced
1/2 Cup water
1 Tbsp goji berries

How to make:

1. Add all the ingredients to a blender and blend until smooth.
2. Enjoy.

(Serves 1)

Calories per serving: 229, Protein: 3g, Carbs: 30g, Fat: 1g

LEMON BOOST

A refreshing drink

Ingredients

2 Tbsp lemon juice
2 Tbsp stevia
4 Pasteurized liquid egg whites
1 Tsp cinnamon

How to make:

1. Add all the ingredients to a blender and blend until smooth.
2. Enjoy.

(Serves 1)

Calories per serving: 79, Protein: 14g, Carbs: 4g, Fat: 1g

GINGER & LEMON GREEN ICED-TEA

Ditch the latte for this energizing drink!

Ingredients

2 Cups concentrated green or macha tea, served hot
1 Lemon, cut into wedges
1/4 Cup crystallized ginger, chopped into fine pieces

How to make:

1. Add all the ingredients to a blender and blend until smooth.
2. Enjoy.

(Serves 1)

Calories per serving: 0, Protein: 0g, Carbs: 0g, Fat: 0g

BANANA & PEANUT MILKSHAKE

A rich shake to fill up on between meals.

Ingredients

2 Tbsp peanut butter (no added sugar or salt)
1 Banana
2 Cups almond milk
1 Tsp raw honey
2 Scoops of vanilla protein powder

How to make:

1. Add all the ingredients to a blender and blend until smooth.
2. Enjoy.

(Serves 1)

Calories per serving: 642, Protein: 48g, Carbs: 48g, Fat: 25g

YOGURT SHAKE

A refreshing drink!

Ingredients

1 Cup Greek Yogurt
1 Tbsp Raw Honey
1/2 Cup Rolled Oats
1 Tbsp Coconut Oil
1 Scoop Of Vanilla Protein Powder

How to make:

1. Add all the ingredients to a blender and blend until smooth.
2. Enjoy.

(Serves 1)

Calories per serving: 402, Protein: 23g, Carbs: 23g, Fat: 23g

DESSERTS

If you want to spend hundreds of pounds on pre-made shakes full of chemicals and fillers that cements onto your kitchen sink then be my guest! If not, try these homemade healthy alternatives that will pack on just as much punch as the shop-bought varieties.

CHOCOLATE & PEANUT PUDDING PIE

A simple and easy recipe to make, this mouth-watering dessert is both cool and creamy. Furthermore, it is packed with a lot of muscle-boosting protein.

Ingredients

1 pack of zero-fat, sugar-free chocolate pudding
1 cup of not-fat milk
2 scoops of chocolate-flavored protein powder
3 tbsp of crunchy peanut butter
Handful of roasted walnuts
2oz of whipped cream
1 piece of chocolate pie crust

How to make:

1. Add all the ingredients to a blender and blend until smooth.
2. Enjoy.

(Serves 4)

Calories per serving: 322, Protein: 20g, Carbs: 20g, Fat: 18g

JASON'S PEANUT PROTEIN BARS

Save your money with these homemade protein bars which taste even better than the shop-bought ones!.

Ingredients

4 scoops of vanilla protein powder
3 cups of rolled oats
12oz of almond butter
1/4 cup of coconut cream

How to make:

1. Get a bowl and add the coconut cream and whisk until smooth, then add the protein powder and peanut butter and mix thoroughly.
2. Pour the oats into the bowl and again mix through.
3. Scoop out the mixture into a baking tray and flatten until the surface is smooth.
4. Place the tray in the fridge and leave for around 8 hours.
5. Cut into 12 bars.

(Makes 12 bars)

Calories per serving: 386, Protein: 18g, Carbs: 24g, Fat: 6g

POWER PARFAIT

A delicious dessert that tastes a great as it looks. Contains a whopping 38g of protein.

Ingredients

1 scoop of vanilla protein powder
2 cups of mixed berries
1/4 cup of Greek yogurt

How to make:

1. Mix the yogurt with the protein powder.
2. Get a tall parfait glass and layer with berries and yogurt.

(Serves 1)

Calories per serving: 254, Protein: 38g, Carbs: 21g, Fat: 2g

STRAWBERRY AND BANANA PROTEIN PUDDING

This is definitely a better alternative to yo-gurt-coated raisins. Though this simple rec-ipe only has a few ingredients, it is certainly not lacking in flavour or nutrients!.

Ingredients

1 scoop of strawberry protein powder
1/4 cup of egg whites
1 tbsp, non-fat, sugar-free chocolate pudding
3 pieces of strawberries, sliced
1 piece of small banana, sliced
Handful of blueberries
2 tbsp of water

How to make:

1. Combine the pudding and protein powder.
2. Add water and egg whites; mix well to achieve thick consistency.
3. Add powder if texture is still runny.
4. Spoon the batter out and transfer to a small plate.
5. Put in the freezer for half an hour.
6. Garnish with the strawberries, banana and blue-berries

(Serves 1)

Calories per serving: 195, Protein: 23g, Carbs: 13g, Fat: 7g

POWER PROTEIN WAFFLES

Who said waffles were unhealthy? These protein waffles even add to your protein goals and are a great alternative to another batch of chicken!.

Ingredients

4 eggs whites
1 scoop of vanilla protein powder
1/2 cup of rolled oats
1 tsp of baking powder
½ tsp of stevia

How to make:

1.   Add all the ingredients into a blender and blend.
2.   Add the mixture to a waffle iron and bake.

(Serves 1)

Calories per serving: 314, Protein: 37g, Carbs: 28g, Fat: 5g

BRAWNY BANANA PROTEIN COOKIES

This recipe is a must try recipe for banana lovers.

Ingredients

2 bananas
1 cup of oatmeal
2 scoop of vanilla protein powder
2 tsp of cinnamon
¼ tsp of baking powder
Handful of finely chopped walnuts or almonds

How to make:

1.   Pre-heat the oven to 1800C/3500F/Gas Mark 4.
2.   Oil-spray a non-stick pan.
3.   Lightly oil-spray a cookie sheet. Distribute the oil evenly using a paper towel.
4.   Get a large-sized bowl and mash the bananas until a creamy texture is achieved.
5.   Add protein powder, oat, salt, walnuts, baking powder, and cinnamon. Mix well. Spoon mixture onto cookie sheet, forming cookie shaped pieces.
6.   Bake for around 15 minutes.
7.   Serve.

(Serves 2)

Calories per serving: 359, Protein: 25g, Carbs: 40g, Fat: 11g

GREEK YOGURT WITH HONEY AND BERRIES

A quick and easy dessert that contains a whopping 43g of protein.

Ingredients

1 scoop of vanilla protein powder
4oz Greek Yoghurt
4 tbsp of honey
1/2 cup of berries

How to make:

1. Mix all your ingredients and you've got a fresh and healthy dessert with nothing on your conscience. You could sprinkle flaked almonds over the top for a bit of crunch.

(Serves 1)

Calories per serving: 522, Protein: 43g, Carbs: 86g, Fat: 7g

POWER PEANUT CHOCOLATE PANCAKES

Sure, you can get your cravings for the peanut butter-chocolate combo through candy bars, but that is not healthy at all. Try this recipe instead....

Ingredients

1 scoop of chocolate protein powder
1 tbsp of smooth peanut butter
2 egg whites
2 tbsp of raw coconut flour

How to make:

1. Get a bowl and combine all ingredients. Mix well until you get a thick batter.
2. Pour the butter on a greased skillet like you would a pancake, frying over a medium heat.
3. Serve when done cooking.

(Serves 2)

Calories per serving: 286, Protein: 33g, Carbs: 16g, Fat: 10g

STRENGTH STRAWBERRY & CHEESE SURPRISE

Another heavenly combination – strawberries and cheese – this is a must-try vegetarian version, especially for muscle builders.

Ingredients

1 cup of low-fat cottage cheese
1 cup of whole strawberries fresh
¼ cup of egg whites
¼ cup of skimmed or soya milk
¾ cup of whole wheat flour
1 packet of stevia
1 ½ tsp of lemon juice

How to make:

1. Combine the milk, flour, and cottage cheese in a mixing bowl.
2. Beat the egg whites separately to achieve a frothy consistency.
3. Gently fold into the cheese mixture.
4. Stir in the lemon juice and toss in the strawberries. Stir again.
5. Transfer the mix into a non-stick frying pan (as you would an omelette) on a medium heat.
6. Turn when the tops start to bubble, and the bottom part starts to turn brown.
7. Serve.

(Serves 4)

Calories per serving: 167, Protein: 15g, Carbs: 20g, Fat: 3g

PROTEIN PUMPKIN COOKIES

Craving for cookies? This easy low-fat recipe is sure to give you a healthy fix to this one!

Ingredients

2 scoops of vanilla protein powder
2 boxes of spice cake mix
2 cups of chocolate chips
(1 can) of pumpkin

How to make:

1. Pre-heat the oven to 1800C/3500F/Gas Mark 4.
2. Combine all ingredients, and gently spoon onto a baking sheet.
3. Bake for about 12 minutes.
4. Serve.

(Serves 4)

Calories per serving: 167, Protein: 15g, Carbs: 20g, Fat: 3g

COTTAGE CHEESECAKE

A hearty, protein packed cheesecake to enjoy!

Ingredients

4oz of fat free cottage cheese
1 scoop of vanilla protein powder
1 packet of stevia
1 tbsp sugar free instant pudding mix
5 tbsp of low fat milk
Handful of strawberries

How to make:

1. Add all the ingredients to a blender and blend until smooth.
2. Place in a bowl and top with the strawberries.
3. Place in the fridge for 20 minutes.
4. Serve and enjoy!

(Serves 1)

Calories per serving: 487, Protein: 43g, Carbs: 53g, Fat: 7g

CRUNCHY APPLE PIE

Oven baked hearty dessert!

Ingredients

2 Cups cooking apples, peeled and sliced
2 Whole cloves
1 Tsp cinnamon
1 Cup whole-wheat breadcrumbs
1/4 Cup hazelnuts, crushed
1 Tbsp coconut oil

How to make:

1. Preheat the oven to 190°C/375°F/Gas Mark 5.
2. Boil a pot of water over a high heat and add the apples, cloves and cinnamon.
3. Turn down the heat slightly and allow to cook for 30-35 minutes or until very soft.
4. Drain and add apples to the bottom of an oven dish.
5. Blitz up the breadcrumbs and hazelnuts and add coconut oil to combine.
6. Top the apples with this mixture and place in the oven to bake for 20-30 minutes or until golden brown

(Serves 4)

Calories per serving: 137, Protein: 2g, Carbs: 20g, Fat: 6g

STRAWBERRY MOUSSE

Try mixing this up for a guilt-free dessert.

Ingredients

2 Cups silken extra firm tofu
2 Tbsp soy milk
3 Scoops strawberry flavoured protein powder
1/2 Cup fresh strawberries

How to make:

1. Blend the tofu and milk until smooth (you can use water here instead if you wish).
2. Now add the protein powder until smooth.
3. Add the mousse into serving cups and cover and refrigerate for 4-5 hours.
4. Enjoy with fresh strawberries.

(Serves 3)

Calories per serving: 236, Protein: 35g, Carbs: 9g, Fat: 8g

PECAN & DARK CHOCOLATE CHIP COOKIES

Wholegrain cookies without the sin.

Ingredients

1 Cup pecans
1 Cup ground flax meal
2 Cups wholegrain rolled oats
1 Tsp nutmeg
1/2 Cup whole wheat flour
1 Tsp baking soda
1/4 Cup stevia
1 Free range egg
1/4 Cup coconut oil
1 Tsp vanilla extract
1 Cup dark chocolate chips
1/2 Cup blueberries
1/2 Cup whole almond butter

How to make:

1. Preheat the oven to 190°C/375°F/Gas Mark 5.
2. Line a baking dish with parchment paper.
3. Grind the walnuts in a blender to make flour.
4. Add all of the other ingredients (except for the almond butter, blueberries and chocolate chips) and process.
5. Add mixture to a bowl and then fold in the chocolate chips and blueberries.
6. Mix the flour mixture into the almond butter until a sticky dough is formed.
7. Use a tablespoon to spoon mini cookie shapes onto your baking tray and bake for 9 minutes before placing them on a wire rack to cool.

(Serves 6)

Calories per serving: 346, Protein: 8g, Carbs: 28g, Fat: 23g

RASPBERRY & VANILLA MUFFINS

Bake these up and enjoy!.

Ingredients

3 Egg whites
1/10 Cup chickpea flour
1 Tbsp coconut flour
1 Tsp of baking powder
1 Tbsp nutmeg, grated
1 Tsp vanilla extract
1 Tsp stevia
1/2 Cup fresh raspberries

How to make:

1. Pre-heat the oven to 325°F/170 °C/Gas Mark 3.
2. Mix all of the ingredients in a mixing bowl.
3. Divide the batter into 4 and spoon into a muffin tin.
4. Bake in the oven for 15-20 minutes or until cooked through.
5. Your knife should pull out clean from the middle of the muffins once done.
6. Allow to cool on a wired rack before serving..

(Serves 4)

Calories per serving: 36, Protein: 4g, Carbs: 4g, Fat: 1g

RAISIN & COCONUT BOOSTERS

Snack on these.

Ingredients

1 Cup Sun-Dried Raisins, Finely Chopped
1/2 Cup Walnuts, Finely Chopped
1/2 Cup Desiccated Coconut
1 Tbsp Honey

How to make:

1. Mix the ingredients together to form a sticky dough.
2. Shape into bite size balls with the palms of your hands.
3. Cover and refrigerate for at least 2 hours to set.
4. Serve or wrap for later.

(Serves 4)

Calories per serving: 241, Protein: 6g, Carbs: 35g, Fat: 10g

VANILLA PANCAKES & APRICOTS

Amazing!

Ingredients

2 Scoops vanilla protein powder
2 Free range egg whites
2 Tbsp of raw coconut flour
1 Tbsp coconut oil
1 Cup greek yogurt
2 Apricots, sliced
1 Tsp nutmeg

How to make:

1. Add all the ingredients to a blender and blend until smooth.
2. Place in a bowl and top with the strawberries.
3. Place in the fridge for 20 minutes.
4. Serve and enjoy!

(Serves 1)

Calories per serving: 487, Protein: 43g, Carbs: 53g, Fat: 7g

CONVERSION TABLES

Volume

Imperial	Metric
1 tbsp	15ml
2 fl oz	55 ml
3 fl oz	75 ml
5 fl oz (¼ pint)	150 ml
10 fl oz (½ pint)	275 ml
1 pint	570 ml
1 ¼ pints	725 ml
1 ¾ pints	1 litre
2 pints	1.2 litres
2½ pints	1.5 litres
4 pints	2.25 litres

Oven temperatures

Gas Mark	Fahrenheit	Celsius
1/4	225	110
1/2	250	130
1	275	140
2	300	150
3	325	170
4	350	180
5	375	190
6	400	200
7	425	220
8	450	230
9	475	240

Weight

Imperial	Metric
½ oz	10 g
¾ oz	20 g
1 oz	25 g
1½ oz	40 g
2 oz	50 g
2½ oz	60 g
3 oz	75 g
4 oz	110 g
4½ oz	125 g
5 oz	150 g
6 oz	175 g
7 oz	200 g
8 oz	225 g
9 oz	250 g
10 oz	275 g
12 oz	350 g

REFERENCES

Schoenfeld, Brad, Alan Aragon, and James W. Krieger. "The Effect of Protein Timing on Muscle Strength and Hypertrophy: A Meta-analysis." J Int Soc Sports Nutr Journal of the International Society of Sports Nutrition 10, no. 1 (2013): 53. doi:10.1186/1550-2783-10-53.

Kumar, V., P. Atherton, K. Smith, and M. J. Rennie. "Human Muscle Protein Synthesis and Breakdown during and after Exercise." Journal of Applied Physiology 106, no. 6 (2009): 2026-039. doi:10.1152/japplphysiol.91481.2008.

Langley-Evans, Simon. "Keith N. Frayn Metabolic Regulation: A Human Perspective, 2nd Ed. Oxford, UK: Blackwell Publishing 2003. P. 339. £24.99 (paperback). ISBN 0-632-06384-X." BJN British Journal of Nutrition 92, no. 06 (2004): 1013. doi:10.1079/bjn20041232.

Rickli, Jonas. "Bodybuilding." Grenzbereiche Der Sportmedizin, 1990, 159-76. doi:10.1007/978-3-642-75429-6_11.

"Understanding Bodybuilding." Science Signaling 2004, no. 239 (2004). doi:10.1126/stke.2392004tw227.

Lacovara, Paul Dominick. Bodybuilding. 2002.

Gilman, Sander L. Diets and Dieting: A Cultural Encyclopedia. New York: Routledge, 2008.

Jacobs, Peter, and Lucille Wood. Macronutrients. St. Louis, MO: Mosby, 2004.

INDEX

Made in the USA
Lexington, KY
10 February 2017